GREEN WOOD
FOR THE GARDEN

GREEN WOOD
FOR THE GARDEN

15 easy weekend projects using freshly cut wood

Alan and Gill Bridgewater

BARRON'S

First published 2002 in the United States and Canada by Barron's Educational Series, Inc.

Text, illustrations, and photographs copyright © 2002 by New Holland Publishers (UK) Ltd. All rights reserved.

Published in the United Kingdom by New Holland Publishers (UK) Ltd.

All inquiries should be addressed to:
Barron's Educational Series, Inc.
250 Wireless Boulevard
Hauppauge, New York 11788
http://www.barronseduc.com

Library of Congress Catalog Card No. 2001094070

International Standard Book No. 0-7641-2156-1

Printed in Malaysia

9 8 7 6 5 4 3 2 1

The information in this book is true and complete to the best of our knowledge. All recommendations are made without
guarantee on the part of the authors and the publishers. The authors and publishers disclaim any liability for damages or injury
resulting from the use of this information.

CONVERSION CHART

The metric measurements given in this book have been converted to imperial measurements by multiplying the metric figure given in the text by the relevant number shown in the table to the right. Bear in mind that conversions will not necessarily work out exactly, and some figures have been slightly rounded up or down. (Do not use a combination of metric and imperial measurements – for accuracy, keep to one system.)

To convert	*Multiply by*
millimeters to inches	0.0394
meters to feet	3.28
meters to yards	1.093
sq millimeters to sq inches	0.00155
sq meters to sq feet	10.76
sq meters to sq yards	1.195
cu meters to cu feet	35.31
cu meters to cu yards	1.308
grams to pounds	0.0022
kilograms to pounds	2.2046
liters to gallons	0.22

CONTENTS

INTRODUCTION

*W*hen *we were first married, we used to enjoy going on day-long rambling walks in the woodlands around our country cottage home. Our memories are of hot days with dappled sunlight shimmering through the trees, and the continual quest for the perfect place for a picnic. One such walk led us deeper and deeper into a great forest, and we became worried about losing our way. Then we pushed through the trees into a sunlit*

Making green wood furniture and other structures for the garden is a creative and therapeutic activity, which anyone can enjoy.

glade, and there in front of us stood a woodcutter's cottage complete with a sawhorse, a log pile, and a mountain of wood shavings.

The whole cottage looked as if had been fashioned out of the forest. The gate was made from rough, split boards, the door latch was a gnarled, forked branch, the bridge over the brook consisted of a couple of fallen trees, the porch posts were tree sections; even the shed was built in the style of a log cabin. Items made from green wood were everywhere – birdhouses, hay rakes, brooms, clothes pegs, porch chairs – all beautifully made from fresh-sawed logs that had been variously split, left in the bark, bent, and shaped with saw, ax, and knife. For us, it was a vision of how life could be, and we were entranced.

From then on, we had a dream to aspire to. We would buy a small woodland lot and build a log cabin cottage. We would have a couple of children, grow our own food, swap our car for a horse, and build our furniture from green wood. Of course, we now know that our dreams were the enthusiasm of young love, but despite that, from that day to this, we have always tried in a modest way to hold true to our romantic vision. Alongside our other home-building activities – including working with stone, designing water gardens, and wood carving – we have, wherever possible, used green wood for building structures.

Working with green wood has various advantages. The basic raw materials are readily available and relatively cheap, and the techniques required are straightforward and easily learned. You don't need a workshop filled with expensive machinery and a wide range of tools. For the projects in this book, you only need a few uncomplicated tools. If you have a garden with a patch of lawn, and a lean-to shelter to store your wood and tools, the rest is simple. Making garden furniture and structures doesn't get any easier than this.

Not so long ago, the practice of working with green wood had fallen out of favor, but it is now an inherent part of the fast-growing popular movement to conserve our native forests. If you like the idea of collecting green wood, splitting it with an ax, cutting basic joints, and then using the items that you have made to embellish your home and garden, you will find this book stimulating and rewarding.

Best of luck.

Alan & Gill

HEALTH AND SAFETY

Many woodworking procedures are potentially dangerous, so before starting work on the projects, read through the following checklist:

☞ Make sure that you are fit and strong enough for the task ahead. If you have any doubts about your health, ask your doctor for advice.

☞ When using an ax, ensure that you are working at a comfortable height, with your legs well braced, and with your hands and legs away from the arc of swing. Check that nobody else is nearby.

☞ Whenever possible, use battery-powered tools rather than those with cables.

☞ Always use a safety electric circuit breaker between the electric outlet and your power tools to protect you from electric shock.

☞ If components or completed sections are heavy, ask friends to help you lift them.

☞ Keep a first aid kit and telephone within easy reach, in case of emergencies.

☞ If your children want to be involved, let them watch at a safe distance, or help with small tasks, but never leave them unsupervised.

ABOUT GREEN WOOD

*I*t's a wonderfully uplifting experience to cut down a section of coppice (or even to buy the wood already cut) and then to convert the posts, poles, rods, and wands into items for the porch and garden. The smell of the sap and the feel of the tools will transport you to the world of a cottage woodsman or that of an American pioneer.

THE HISTORY OF GREEN WOOD

Green wood is freshly cut wood that is still in its wet or "green" state, as opposed to dried, seasoned wood. Traditionally, a woodsman used wood not long after it had been cut, whereas a carpenter worked with prepared sections. Working with tools such as a saw, ax, and drawknife, woodsmen converted trees and coppice into everything from gates and fence hurdles to rakes, scythe handles, clogs, chairs, brooms, hoops, and tent pegs.

Unfortunately, since the timber trade was mechanized in the 1940s (allowing whole trees to be mechanically dried, sliced up, and run out as standard sections), green wood activity has, to a great extent, fallen into decline. However, the good news is that there is currently a revival of interest in green wood products, with a new generation of craftspeople making everything from porch chairs to benches, garden shelters, gates, birdhouses, screens, hurdles, trugs, and orchard ladders.

MATERIALS

Green wood, the basic raw material, can be obtained as large-section timber in the form of rough-sawed boards or split posts and rails, and as small-section coppice wood in the form of poles, rods, and wands. Large-section timber is obtained by felling whole trees and sawing the trunk into planks and boards, while small-section coppice wood is produced by cutting certain trees back to ground level, and then using the cluster of straight growth that springs up from the tree bole.

The definitions of words used to describe coppice, such as post and pole, vary according to region, so the best thing to do is to go to the supplier armed with a list of sizes. An added complication is the fact that coppice wood is, by its very nature, thicker at one end than at the other. For the projects in this book, our definitions are as follows. Wands range in diameter from $\frac{1}{5}$ in. to $\frac{3}{5}$ in. (5 mm to 15 mm), rods from $\frac{3}{5}$ in. to $1\frac{1}{2}$ in. (15 mm to 40 mm), poles from $1\frac{1}{2}$ in. to 3 in. (40 mm to 80 mm), and posts from 3 in. to 6 in. (80 mm to 150 mm).

All green wood, from large sections to small sections, should be purchased from managed woodlands that are carefully cropped and tended, rather than woodlands that are stripped and then left. Using green wood in this way shows a respect for nature – it's the right and proper way to use wood to its best potential in your area. Other materials such as nails, wire, and twine can be obtained from home improvement stores.

A coppice woodland. The growth from the bole of trees that have been coppiced (cut back to ground level) is used for small-section green wood such as poles, rods, and wands, ranging from $\frac{1}{5}$ in. to 3 in. (5 mm to 80 mm) in diameter.

Green wood and other materials for making projects (other species of wood may be used). **(1)** *Sawed green plank.* **(2)** *Hazel rods.* **(3)** *Mixed poles.* **(4)** *Beech coppice rods.* **(5)** *Larch post.* **(6)** *Chopping log.* **(7)** *Galvanized nails.* **(8)** *Steel nails.* **(9)** *De-barked larch post.* **(10)** *Holly wands.* **(11)** *Natural twine.* **(12)** *Galvanized wire.*

TOOLS

Working with green wood isn't an exact science. Because of its random nature (loose bark, tapering sections, knots, and all types of bends and twists), a lot of the measuring, marking, and cutting can be done by eye. So study the unique shapes of your wood, measure and cut generously oversize, and then trim back to best fit. All the tools featured here are available from home improvement stores.

TOOLS FOR MEASURING AND MARKING

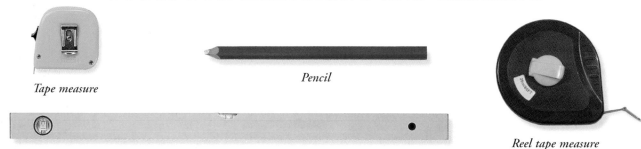

Tape measure

Pencil

Reel tape measure

Spirit level

You need two types of rulers for measuring: a large, flexible reel tape measure for setting out site plans and for measuring lengths and girths, and a flexible metal measure for all the general sizing. If you can afford the extra cost, choose a fiberglass reel tape measure, because they are durable, don't buckle or snap, and it doesn't matter if they get wet. You will also need a good size spirit level and a supply of carpenter's flat-lead pencils. Buy the cheapest spirit level available and then you won't be too upset if it gets crushed.

TOOLS FOR CUTTING WOOD

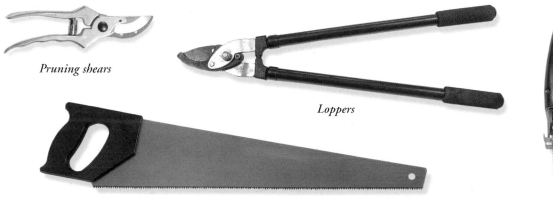

Pruning shears

Loppers

Jigsaw

Crosscut saw

You need a general-purpose, coarse-toothed crosscut saw for cutting boards, posts, poles, and thick rods; a pair of long-handled loppers for cutting thin rods and thick wands; hand pruning shears for cutting thin wands; and a power jigsaw for cutting curves in boards. Because green wood is generally wet, gritty, bark-covered, knotty, and sticky with sap and resin, we recommend that you purchase top-quality loppers and pruning shears (because they can be cleaned and sharpened easily) and cheap, throwaway saws.

TOOLS FOR MAKING JOINTS

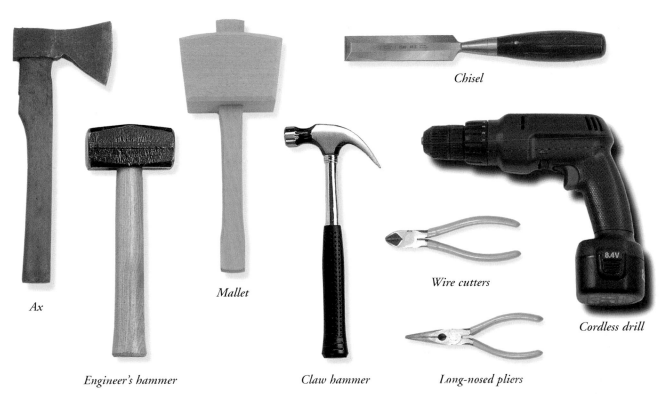

Chisel

Wire cutters

Cordless drill

Ax

Mallet

Engineer's hammer

Claw hammer

Long-nosed pliers

You need eight basic tools for making joints in green wood. We use a small ax for rough shaping and stripping off bark, a mallet and chisel for making precise cuts, a cordless drill for drilling pilot holes prior to nailing, a claw hammer for pounding in nails, an engineer's hammer for use as an anvil when clenching over the points of nails, wire cutters, and pliers. If you decide to use a power drill, make sure that you use it in conjunction with a safety electric circuit breaker. Choose a good-quality ax – we use a hand-forged black iron ax, made in China. It didn't cost much; nevertheless it is a top-quality tool. It is just the right weight, the blade is thin and double-beveled, and the handle is well shaped, made from straight-grained wood and comfortable to hold. If you need to cut costs, it may be possible to purchase secondhand tools from a garage sale or flea market.

OTHER USEFUL TOOLS

You need a pair of portable workbenches for most sawing and jointing tasks, a chopping log when using the ax, and a stepladder for high-reach projects such as the "Tea for Two" Shelter. For one or two of the projects you will also require a garden spade for leveling sites and digging holes for posts, a standard sledgehammer for pounding in posts, and a piece of $3/4$ in.- (20 mm-) thick, exterior-grade plywood for use as a ground-level workboard.

GREEN WOOD TECHNIQUES

W*orking with green wood in the garden is an enjoyable activity to undertake. Anyone who can hold a saw, trim bark with an ax, and pound in a nail is capable of making all the projects. If you are ready to let the natural shape of the wood be your guide, you will find that the techniques are as easy as . . . falling off a log.*

MEASURING AND MARKING

Much of the measuring is best done by eye. Hold the wood in place, mark the line with the saw, and then make the cut.

When working with unevenly shaped wood, a spirit level can only give an overall estimation of the accuracy of horizontal positioning.

Marking out
Use a tape measure, pegs, and string to establish the size and position of the structure

Squareness
To ensure that the shape has 90° corners, the diagonals must be an identical length

Peg out a rectangle, with opposite sides of equal length. Measure the distance between the diagonals at each end, add the measurements together, and divide by two. Adjust the pegs so that both diagonals conform to this measurement.

These procedures of measuring and marking are carried out with a tape measure, spirit level, and your eyes. We usually measure and cut the component parts so that they are oversize, and then make final adjustments by eye. When working with green wood and testing with the measure and spirit level, you have to go for the best overall fit and squareness. (A good way of testing the accuracy of a square or a rectangle is to make adjustments until the diagonal measurements are identical.)

When using green wood, you have to work with round sections that are, to various extents, tapered, bent, and twisted. You have to be flexible in your approach, and remember that the whole essence and character of green wood forms are that they are less than perfect.

SAWING, LOPPING, AND AXING

Use a general-purpose, coarse-toothed saw for making straight cuts in slabs of wood and for cutting large-diameter, round-section wood (greater than ³/₄ in. [20 mm] in diameter).

Curved shapes
A jigsaw's narrow blade allows you to guide the saw along curved lines

When you need to cut out curved shapes from slabs of wood, use an electric jigsaw. Fit a blade with teeth of a size that relates to the thickness of the material you are cutting. A jigsaw is not suitable for cutting round-section wood.

Normally, we advocate using quality traditional tools for most jobs; however, sawing green wood is one of the few tasks that is best achieved with a cheap, general-purpose, coarse-toothed saw. The reason is that the wet, sappy, resinous wood is so hard on the teeth that a saw only lasts for a couple of projects. Whether using a hand saw or a jigsaw, we usually do the sawing close to where the project will be sited, with the workpiece either leaning against, or clamped in, the portable workbench.

When it comes to cutting rods and wands, you have to decide whether to use long-handled loppers or pruning shears. Although much depends upon the hardness of the wood being worked, we usually choose loppers for thick wood and pruning shears for thin wands. When using the loppers, you will find it much easier to cut at a low angle, so that you make a long, low, shearing cut angled to the run of the grain.

When using an ax, you need a chopping block to work on. A tree stump measuring approximately 16 in. (400 mm) in diameter and 24 in. (600 mm) high is ideal. When making a glancing cut – as you might do when pointing a post or shaving off an area of bark – nail a strip of wood across the chopping block to act as a stop. This will prevent the piece of work from sliding away from the ax. It is better to use several light, well-aimed blows to shape the wood you are working on, rather than attempting to shape the wood with one blow, which frequently results in taking off more than you intended.

Use a pair of loppers for cutting small-section wood to length (wands and rods between ³/₈–³/₄ in. [10–20 mm] in diameter).

Axing
Take several shavings to achieve the shape you want

Chopping block
You will need a block to support the workpiece

A sharp ax is ideal for carving wood to shape. Use it to create pointed or flattened ends on rods and poles.

CUTTING JOINTS

To make an angled half-lap joint, clamp the post in a vise and start by sawing halfway through its thickness.

Using an ax like a chisel, hit it with a piece of wood to split out the waste from the half-lap joint.

To level a section of a component in preparation for jointing, use a broad chisel to shave away the wood.

Jointing green wood involves taking two or more component parts – posts, poles, rods, or wands – and attaching them together so that they become a strong and stable whole. However, the thing that makes green wood jointing so challenging is the fact that the components are randomly round in cross-section and tapered in length. In general terms, there are two ways of creating a joint. You can butt the two parts together bark to bark, in which case there is very little contact between the components and the joint ends up being relatively weak. Alternatively, you can use a combination of saw, ax, and chisel to cut part of the rounded surfaces of the components to a level finish before butting them together. The leveling option results in a stronger joint.

BENDING AND WEAVING

Bending
The wood must be bent around the curve gently so that it does not break

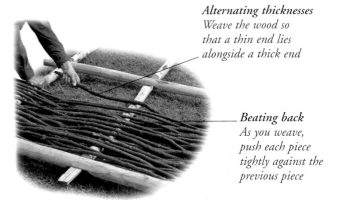

Alternating thicknesses
Weave the wood so that a thin end lies alongside a thick end

Beating back
As you weave, push each piece tightly against the previous piece

Wands of wood can be carefully bent around a curve provided that the wood has been harvested recently.

Weaving wood in and out of a frame (or posts stuck in the ground) creates an attractive screen, border, or fence.

Projects such as the Country Club Chair (see page 66), Warp and Weft Woven Border (see page 30), and Hearts and Diamonds Screen (see page 58), require wood that can be bent. Depending on the project, it may be better to use a thin wand that can be bent easily into a tight circle, as in the Classical Cone project (see page 34), or wood that can be bent into a broad curve, as for the chair and the screen. While many types of wood can be bent, we favor using holly for tight curves, and young hazel and beech for broad curves. Wood harvested in the spring bends more easily than wood cut in winter. Always use local wood from a renewable resource.

DRILLING AND NAILING

Before nailing (especially near the end of a piece of wood) drill a hole through the top piece of wood.

If the work bounces around when you are trying to nail, use an engineer's hammer to help support the wood.

For added strength, use a nail that is long enough to go through both components, then bend the end over.

Once the wood has been cut and jointed, the joint has to be nailed. Depending upon the situation, the nail might run through one component and partially into another, or right through both components.

Always drill pilot holes prior to nailing, to minimize the risk of splitting the wood. Use a drill bit that is slightly smaller than the diameter of your chosen nail. If a joint's strength and stability are crucial to the project, you can go one step further. First, drill right through both components. Using an extra-long nail, hammer it all the way through both pieces of wood so that the point sticks out of the other side. Finally, clench the end of the nail down against the workpiece, or if possible, bend it over so that the point re-enters the wood.

BINDING

Natural twine
Use string or twine made from natural materials

Flexible wood
Green holly is woven into a hoop or "quoit"

Wired joint
Use three loops of wire for each joint

A binding of green wood can be added to a twine binding, to strengthen the joint and improve its appearance.

Wired joints are employed when the wood is too thin to nail successfully. Loops of wire are tightened with pliers.

We use thin, galvanized wire for binding jointed bent wood where there is a lot of stress on the joints created by springing one length of wood against another; string or twine for binding bundles, as in the Obelisk project (see page 42); and thin holly wands for binding items such as the wreaths used in the Classical Cone project (see page 34). When gathering holly, go for the new green growth, rather than last year's wood, as it's both easy to cut and supple. Always seek the owner's permission before helping yourself to wood.

THE
PROJECTS

*In the lists of materials, the
measurements given for length refer
to the wood as you would buy or
harvest it. The measurements
specified for the diameter of sticks
should be treated as a guide.*

BEEHIVE CLOCHE

R*eminiscent of the glass bell, or cloche, that was popular with gardeners in Victorian and Edwardian times, this beautifully decorative woven beehive cloche will both protect and shape young plants. Place the beehive over tender shoots or flowers to provide a barrier that is attractive to look at and perfect for keeping pets and children at bay.*

YOU WILL NEED

Materials for a beehive cloche approximately 24 in. (600 mm) high and 39 in. (1 m) in diameter.

☞ Beech coppice: 8 rods, 9 ft 9 in. (3 m) long and $^3/_5$ in. (15 mm) in diameter (arches, hoops, and diagonal ties)

☞ Logs: 4 short logs about 4 in. (100 mm) in diameter

☞ Galvanized wire: small roll of soft $^1/_{16}$ in. (1 mm) wire

☞ Steel nails: 6 in. (9 x 150 mm)

☞ Ball of thin cotton twine or cord

☞ Ball of coarse natural fiber twine (as used to tie up plants)

Tools

☞ Pencil and flexible ruler

☞ Pliers

☞ Wire cutters

☞ Long-handled loppers

☞ Pruning shears

PERSPECTIVE VIEW OF THE BEEHIVE CLOCHE

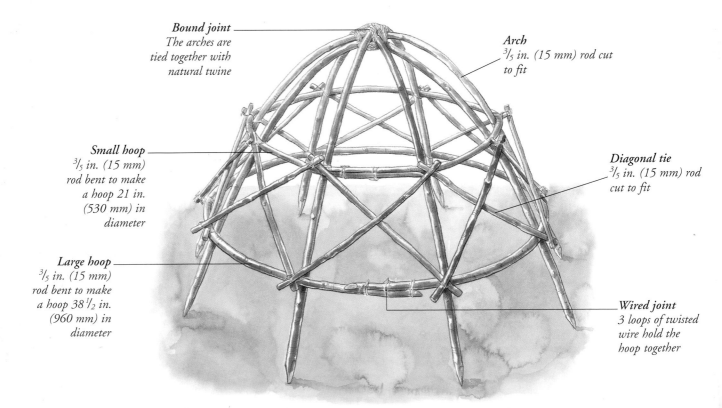

Bound joint
The arches are tied together with natural twine

Arch
$^3/_5$ in. (15 mm) rod cut to fit

Small hoop
$^3/_5$ in. (15 mm) rod bent to make a hoop 21 in. (530 mm) in diameter

Diagonal tie
$^3/_5$ in. (15 mm) rod cut to fit

Large hoop
$^3/_5$ in. (15 mm) rod bent to make a hoop 38 $^1/_2$ in. (960 mm) in diameter

Wired joint
3 loops of twisted wire hold the hoop together

HOW TO MAKE THE BEEHIVE CLOCHE

1 Gently ease and bend the straightest, most flexible beech rod to make a hoop 38½ in. (960 mm) in diameter. Bind the overlapping ends of the rod together with three wire ties. Check that the structure is secure and trim the ends of the rod. Repeat this procedure to make a second hoop 21 in. (530 mm) in diameter.

2 Set the large hoop on the grass, resting it on the four short logs. Push nails in the grass at the center of the hoop and around the edge, just like the points of a compass. Link the nails with ties of thin cotton twine so that the circle is divided into eight wedges. The twine marks the position of the arches.

3 Trim a beech rod to a length of 6½ ft (2 m) and bend it into an arch. Push the ends of the arch into the grass on the inside of the hoop, so that it bridges the diameter of the circle. Continue pushing the ends of the rod into the grass until the peak of the arch stands about 19½ in. (500 mm) high from the grass.

4 Make three other arches as described in Step 3, in order to create the characteristic beehive shape. Use wire to lash the arches securely to the hoop. Ease the ends of the arched rods out of the grass and remove the logs, twine, and nails. Trim the ends of the arches so that the beehive stands 24 in. (600 mm) high.

5 Bind the topmost intersection of the arches with coarse twine so that you finish up with a large, ball-like knot that holds the structure together securely. Drop the second hoop over the beehive, level it by eye, and lash it in place with wire.

6 Trim offcuts of beech rod to fit diagonally across the eight "windows" framed between the two hoops and the curves of the arches. Hold them in place with wire. Finally, trim all the ends of the wood and wire with pruning shears and wire cutters.

DESIGN VARIATIONS

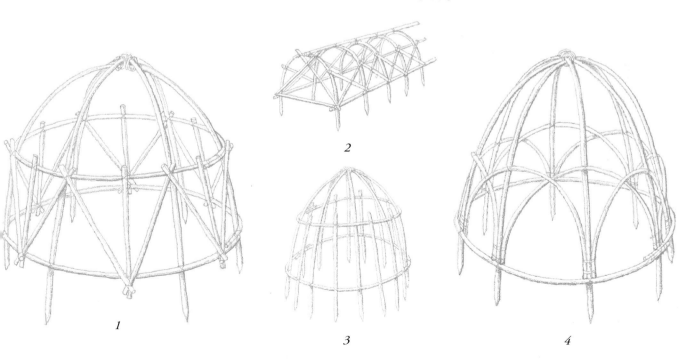

1

2

3

4

(1) A simple cloche with straight, zigzag bracing struts. (2) A seed-bed tunnel made from a number of hoops and *straight bracing struts. (3) A cloche with closely spaced, pet-proof bars. (4) A cloche with bent hoop bracing.*

ARCHED TREFOIL TRELLIS

This delicate trellis was inspired by the spidery rustic woodwork that was favored in the late nineteenth century, especially in cottage gardens. The diamond lattice and the trefoil tracery infill at the top of the Roman arch combine to make a beautifully subtle garden feature, which is perfect for twining with roses or using as a backdrop to add vertical interest to a flower border.

YOU WILL NEED

Materials for a trellis approximately 7 $\frac{1}{2}$ ft (2.34 m) high and 33 $\frac{1}{2}$ in. (850 mm) wide.

- Beech coppice: 4 poles, 6 $\frac{1}{2}$ ft (2 m) long and 1 in. (25 mm) in diameter (main frame)

- Beech coppice: 6 rods, 6 $\frac{1}{2}$ ft (2 m) long and $\frac{3}{4}$ in. (20 mm) in diameter (lattice ties)

- Beech: 3 wands, 6 $\frac{1}{2}$ ft (2 m) long and $\frac{3}{5}$ in. (15 mm) in diameter (arch)

- Holly: 3 wands, 39 in. (1 m) long and $\frac{2}{5}$ in. (10 mm) in diameter (trefoil decoration)

- Galvanized nails: 2 lb (1 kg) box of 3 in. (75 mm x 3.75 mm)

- Galvanized wire: small roll of soft $\frac{1}{16}$ in. (1 mm) wire

Tools

- Pencil and flexible ruler
- Long-handled loppers
- Plywood workboard
- Cordless drill
- Drill bits to match the size of your nails
- Claw hammer
- Engineer's hammer
- Pliers
- Wire cutters
- Pruning shears

FRONT VIEW
OF THE TRELLIS

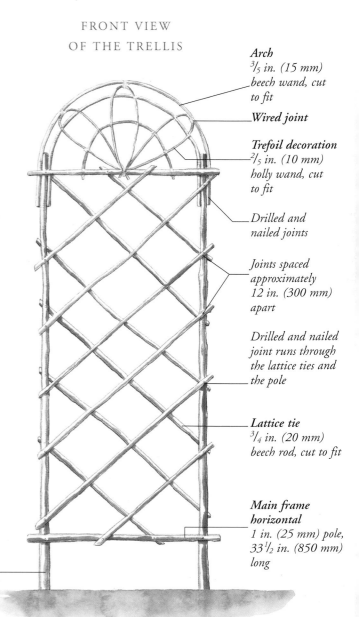

Arch
$\frac{3}{5}$ in. (15 mm) beech wand, cut to fit

Wired joint

Trefoil decoration
$\frac{2}{5}$ in. (10 mm) holly wand, cut to fit

Drilled and nailed joints

Joints spaced approximately 12 in. (300 mm) apart

Drilled and nailed joint runs through the lattice ties and the pole

Lattice tie
$\frac{3}{4}$ in. (20 mm) beech rod, cut to fit

Main frame horizontal
1 in. (25 mm) pole, 33 $\frac{1}{2}$ in. (850 mm) long

Main frame vertical
1 in. (25 mm) beech pole, 6 $\frac{1}{2}$ ft (2 m) long

HOW TO MAKE THE ARCHED TREFOIL TRELLIS

1 Cut the three beech poles for the main frame to length with the loppers, making two at 6½ ft (2 m) (for the verticals) and two at 33½ in. (850 mm) (for the horizontals). Set the verticals flat on the workboard, so that they are parallel and 27 in. (674 mm) apart. Drill and nail the two horizontals in place – one 12 in. (300 mm) up from the bottom and the other about 4 in. (100 mm) down from the top. Turn the frame over and use the claw hammer to bend the points of the nails over.

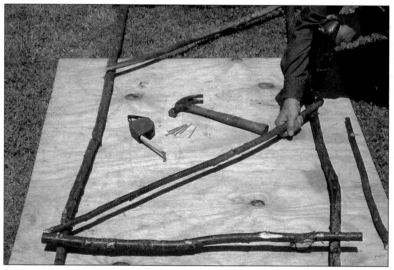

2 Mark off the vertical poles at intervals of 12 in. (300 mm), and mark center-points on the two horizontals as a guide for attaching the lattice. Position the ³/₄ in.- (20 mm-) diameter beech rods for the six diagonal lattice ties on one side of the main frame. Use the loppers to trim the rods to length. Drill and nail the intersections.

3 When you have attached the lattice ties on one side of the main frame, turn the frame over and repeat the procedure on the other side, using the remaining six diagonal lattice ties to form the diamond pattern of the lattice. Use the two hammers to clench the points of the nails: place the nail head on the head of the engineer's hammer (using it like an anvil) and with the claw hammer, bend the point of the nail around and down so that it re-enters the wood.

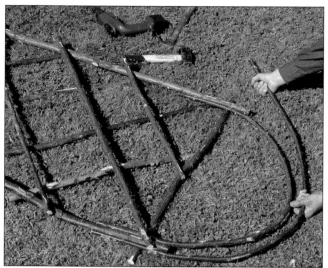

4 Take two of the ³/₅ in.- (15 mm-) diameter beech wands and bend them repeatedly until they are supple and flexible. One piece at a time, drill and nail one end at the top of one side of the frame. Bend the wand over to make a pleasing symmetrical arch and then drill and nail the other end to the other side.

5 Bend the three holly wands until they are flexible. Loop them so that the ends cross, and bind the intersections with wire. Fit the three loops within the arch and wire them in place. Finally, use the last beech wand to make the lower inner arch, wiring it in place. Neaten ends with the pruning shears.

DESIGN VARIATIONS

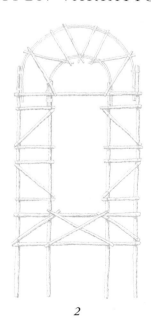

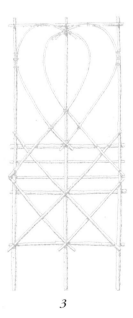

1

2

3

(1) A pediment trellis (with a simple triangular top) can be made entirely from straight components. (2) This Classical-style trellis has an arched top (as in this project) with a column at either side. (3) A trellis reminiscent of American folk art. This is more complex and uses heart and diamond motifs to both decorate and brace the structure.

BIRDHOUSE FEEDER

T*his visually exciting garden feature will attract lots of birds to the garden, with the added advantage that the birds will help you rid the garden of all types of insect pests. Our design echoes an original Victorian feeder that we once saw in a gamekeeper's cottage garden. It is beautiful in its massive simplicity, made from rough-sawed slab wood throughout. The whole structure is held together with nails.*

YOU WILL NEED

Materials for a birdhouse feeder approximately 22 in. (560 mm) high and 27$\frac{1}{2}$ in. (700 mm) wide.

☞ Hardwood (rough-sawed, with waney edges kept intact): 39 in. x 9 ft. 9 in. (1 x 3 m) length, 19$\frac{5}{8}$ in. (500 mm) wide and $\frac{3}{4}$ in. (20 mm) thick (floor, under-floor, walls, roof, wall fixing strips)

☞ Beech coppice: 2 poles, 6$\frac{1}{2}$ ft (2 m) long and 1–1$\frac{1}{2}$ in. (30–40 mm) in diameter (ridge pole, roof finials, and cladding for the side walls)

☞ Larch feature post: about 6$\frac{1}{2}$ ft (2 m) long and 4 in. (100 mm) in diameter, with a fork at the top end (mounting post)

☞ Galvanized nails: 2 lb (1 kg) box of 3 in. (75 mm x 2.65 mm)

☞ Galvanized cap-end roofing nails: 3 in. (2 x 75 mm)

☞ Steel screws: 2 in. (4 x 50 mm) no. 8

Tools

☞ Pencil, flexible ruler, square, and spirit level

☞ Portable workbench

☞ Electric jigsaw

☞ Cordless drill

☞ Wood bits to fit the various nail sizes

☞ Claw hammer

☞ General-purpose, coarse-toothed saw

☞ Small ax

☞ Chopping log

☞ Screwdriver

☞ Spade

PERSPECTIVE VIEW OF THE BIRDHOUSE FEEDER

Roof finial
1–1$\frac{1}{2}$ in. (30–40 mm) beech pole, 6 in. (150 mm) long

Ridge pole
1–1$\frac{1}{2}$ in. (30–40 mm) beech pole, 19 in. (480 mm) long

Roof
$\frac{3}{4}$ in. (20 mm) hardwo[od] 16 in. (480 mm) long [and] 12 in. (310 mm) wide

Doorway
10$\frac{1}{4}$ in. (260 mm) high and 8 in. (200 mm) wide

Cladding
1–1$\frac{1}{2}$ in. (30– beech pole, 12 (310 mm) long

Side wall
$\frac{3}{4}$ in. (20 mm) hardwood, 9$\frac{1}{2}$ in. (239 mm) high and 12 in. (310 mm) wide

Wall fixing strip
$\frac{3}{4}$ in. (20 mm) hardwood, 12 in. (310 mm) long and $\frac{3}{4}$ in. (20 mm) square

Mounting post
4 in. (100 mm) larch post, 6$\frac{1}{2}$ ft (2 m) long, with forked branches at the top

Front gable wall
$\frac{3}{4}$ in. (20 mm) hardwood, 14$\frac{1}{4}$ in. (360 mm) square

Floor
$\frac{3}{4}$ in. (20 mm) hardwood, 27$\frac{1}{2}$ in. (700 mm) wide and 15$\frac{3}{4}$ in. (400 mm) deep. The $\frac{3}{4}$ in. (20 mm) hardwood under-floor piece, hidden from view, is 12 in. (300 mm) square.

HOW TO MAKE THE BIRDHOUSE FEEDER

1 Lay out the floor, under-floor, side walls, front and back gable walls, roof slabs (waney edges left intact), and the strips for attaching the walls to the floor. Cut out the parts with the jigsaw.

2 Drill and nail the gable walls directly to the side walls. The positioning doesn't need to be too exact, as long as the four walls are square to each other, so that the house sits square and firm.

3 Nail the two wall fixing strips in place on the floor slab, so they are 9$\frac{1}{2}$ in. (240 mm) apart on the outside edges. (Drill pilot holes through the strips first, in order to avoid splitting the wood.)

4 Position the two roof slabs directly on top of the gable walls, so that the underside faces of the slabs meet along the line of the ridge, and the edges are well aligned. Drill and nail them in place, with the nails centered in the thickness of the wall.

5 Cut the remaining poles into 12 in. (310 mm) lengths, then with the ax, split them carefully along their length. Drill and nail these half-log sections on the side walls. Make the finials by trimming two waste pieces of beech coppice with the ax.

6 Cut the ridge pole for the roof to length, and then drill and nail it in place with the two cap-end roofing nails, inserting the nails so that they run down into the top edges of the front and back gable walls. Drill and nail the finials to the ends of the ridge pole.

7 Drill and nail the under-floor slab directly to the top of the forked mounting post, and then sit the house on the slab and run screws up from the underside. Dig a hole and erect the mounting post, siting it away from structures that could give cats easy access.

DESIGN VARIATIONS

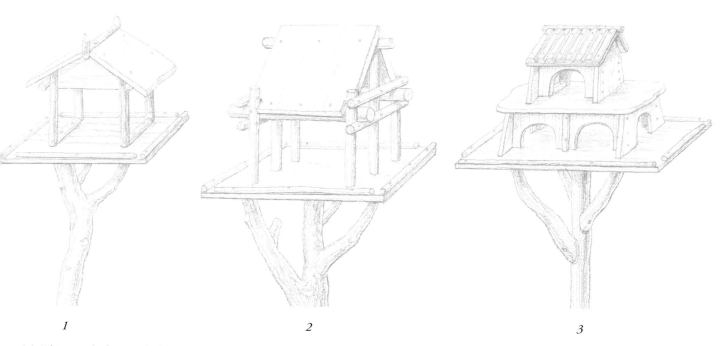

1

2

3

(1) This simple four-stick design is very easy to clean.
(2) Design based on a tribal hut in New Guinea.

(3) A two-story design incorporating arches, with a straight mounting post and added bracketing pieces for support.

WARP AND WEFT WOVEN BORDER

*S*tore-bought woven hurdles and garden screens undoubtedly have their merits, but making your own woven in-bark wood items produces a much more natural effect than factory-sawed laths and slats. It is also possible to build structures to fit the unique shape of your garden. All you do is pound in the warp poles, so that about half their length is in the ground, and then weave the weft rods in and out to make the infill.

YOU WILL NEED

Materials for a woven border approximately 12 in. (300 mm) high and 16$\frac{1}{2}$ ft (5 m) long.

- Mature beech coppice: 3 poles, 6$\frac{1}{2}$ ft (2 m) long and 1$\frac{1}{2}$–2 in. (40–50 mm) in diameter (vertical posts – warp)

- Beech coppice: 16 rods, 6$\frac{1}{2}$ ft (2 m) long and $\frac{2}{5}$–$\frac{3}{5}$ in. (10–15 mm) in diameter (woven infill – weft)

- Galvanized nails: 2 lb (1 kg) box of 3 in. (75 mm x 3.75 mm)

Tools

- Pencil and flexible ruler
- Portable workbench
- General-purpose, coarse-toothed saw

- Chopping log
- Small ax
- Sledgehammer
- Claw hammer
- Long-handled loppers
- Engineer's hammer

PERSPECTIVE VIEW OF THE WOVEN BORDER

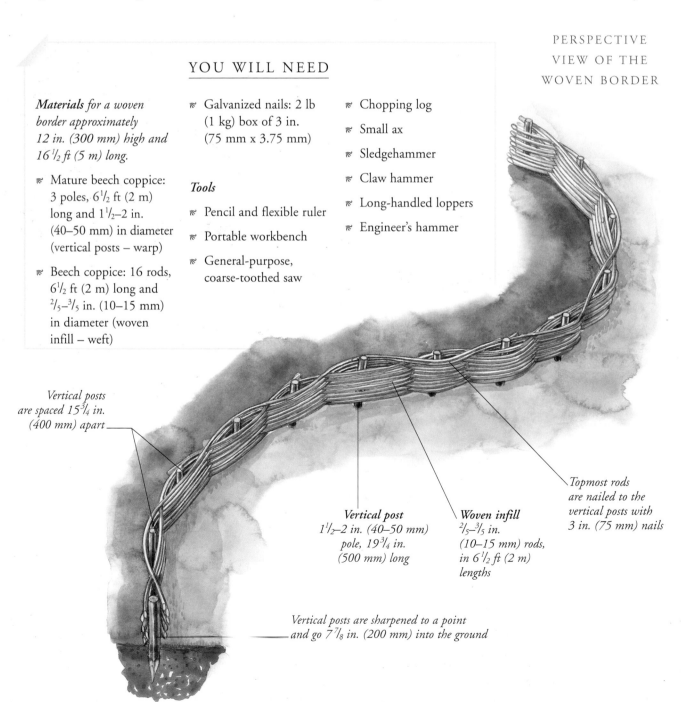

Vertical posts are spaced 15$\frac{3}{4}$ in. (400 mm) apart

Vertical post 1$\frac{1}{2}$–2 in. (40–50 mm) pole, 19$\frac{3}{4}$ in. (500 mm) long

Woven infill $\frac{2}{5}$–$\frac{3}{5}$ in. (10–15 mm) rods, in 6$\frac{1}{2}$ ft (2 m) lengths

Topmost rods are nailed to the vertical posts with 3 in. (75 mm) nails

Vertical posts are sharpened to a point and go 7$\frac{7}{8}$ in. (200 mm) into the ground

HOW TO MAKE THE WOVEN BORDER

1 Saw the three 6½ ft- (2 m-) long beech poles into quarters to make vertical posts about 19¾ in. (500 mm) long. Next, shape one end of each post to a point. Set the chopping log at a comfortable working height. Nail a piece of scrap wood to the log to act as a stop. Butt a post up against the stop, and use the ax to sharpen its end to a point. Repeat for the other posts.

2 Cut a 15¾ in.- (400 mm-) long measuring stick from a piece of waste wood to use as a spacer to mark the distance between the vertical posts along the length of the woven border. Take the sledgehammer and pound the vertical posts into the ground to a depth of about 8 in. (200 mm), so that they stand 12 in. (300 mm) high. Be careful not to split the posts.

3 Taking one beech rod at a time, weave it in and out of the vertical posts to form the woven infill. The characteristic pattern is achieved by alternating the rods so that the thick end of one rod is set against the thin end of another.

4 When you come to join rods, use the loppers to trim the end of the old rod close to the post it has just cleared. If possible, join the new rods so that the thick ends overlap the thin. They do not need to be nailed.

5 As you work, beat the rods down so that they fit together in both plan and front view. Spend time choosing the rods you use, so that the various dips and bends of the wood mesh together for a close fit and pleasing appearance.

6 Finally, when you have woven as many rods as possible into the 12 in. (300 mm) height of the vertical posts, use the claw hammer, as shown, to nail the topmost rods to the vertical posts. Use the engineer's hammer to support the post while nailing.

DESIGN VARIATIONS

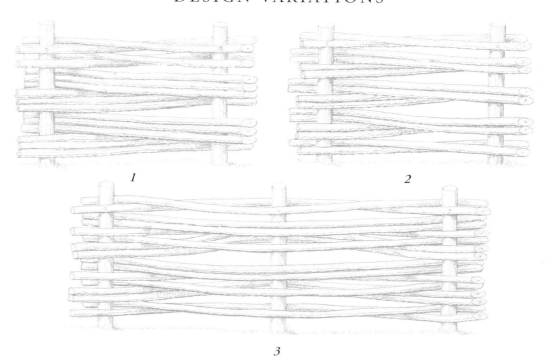

1

2

3

(1) A simple design with four sticks woven normally at the top, and the other sticks woven in groups of three.

(2) Another design using groups of two sticks. *(3)* A more complicated design with the appearance of a random pattern.

CLASSICAL CONE

O*f all the geometric motifs traditionally used in gardens, such as obelisks, cubes, and spheres, the cone has long been the most popular, from carved stone cones on plinths to yew trees sculpted into dramatic, giant freestanding cones. If you would like a green wood cone to grace your garden – as a frame for a climbing plant, or simply as a design statement – this one can be made quickly and easily.*

YOU WILL NEED

***Materials** for a cone approximately 6 $\frac{1}{2}$ ft (2 m) high and 24 in. (600 mm) in diameter.*

- Holly: 12 wands, 6 $\frac{1}{2}$ ft (2 m) long and $\frac{2}{5}$ in. (10 mm) in diameter (quoits)

- Beech coppice: 16 poles, 6 $\frac{1}{2}$ ft (2 m) long and 1 in. (25 mm) in diameter (verticals)

- Galvanized wire: small roll of soft $\frac{1}{16}$ in. (1 mm) wire

- Ball of coarse natural fiber twine (as used to tie up plants)

Tools

- Pencil and flexible ruler

- Long-nosed pliers

- Scissors

- Long-handled loppers

- Pruning shears

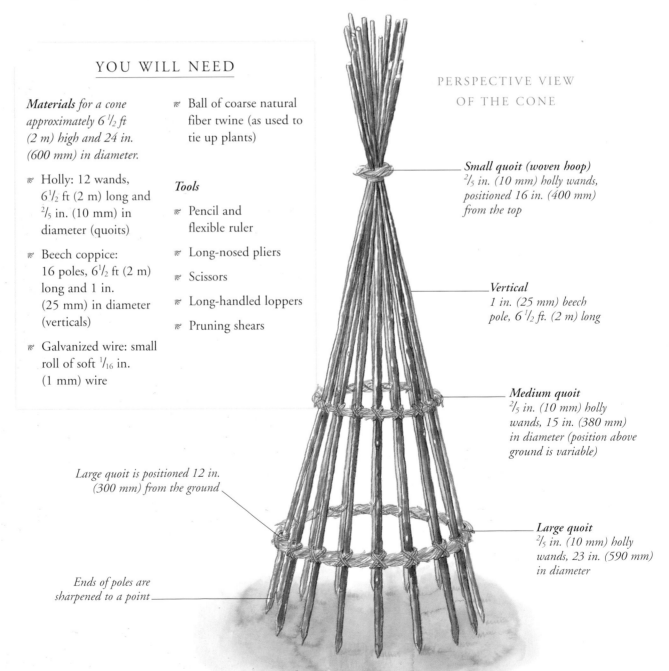

PERSPECTIVE VIEW OF THE CONE

Small quoit (woven hoop) $\frac{2}{5}$ *in. (10 mm) holly wands, positioned 16 in. (400 mm) from the top*

Vertical *1 in. (25 mm) beech pole, 6 $\frac{1}{2}$ ft. (2 m) long*

Medium quoit $\frac{2}{5}$ *in. (10 mm) holly wands, 15 in. (380 mm) in diameter (position above ground is variable)*

Large quoit $\frac{2}{5}$ *in. (10 mm) holly wands, 23 in. (590 mm) in diameter*

Large quoit is positioned 12 in. (300 mm) from the ground

Ends of poles are sharpened to a point

HOW TO MAKE THE CLASSICAL CONE

1 First, make the large quoit, or woven hoop. Gently flex the strongest holly wand over your knee to create a rough hoop measuring about 23 in. (590 mm) in diameter, and allowing a good overlap at the two ends. Wrap three bindings of wire over the overlap, one at each end and one in the middle, tightening them with the pliers.

2 Take some of the softer, more flexible lengths of holly and wind them in and around the basic hoop until you have a large, fat quoit resembling a Christmas wreath. Wire the ends as necessary. Repeat the procedure to make the medium quoit measuring 15 in. (380 mm) in diameter.

3 Set the large quoit on the grass and push the sixteen 6½ ft (2 m) beech poles into the ground around it, positioning them at the eight compass points, and at the eight points between these.

4 Lift the quoit upright, then pull it out through the beech poles. Gather the poles at a point about 15 in. (400 mm) from the top, and bind them with twine. Take the remaining lengths of holly wand and wind them in and around the bound area to cover the twine and make the small quoit.

5 Drop the large quoit over the cone and ease it into a position about 12 in. (300 mm) above the ground. Wind and tie twine over each of the sixteen intersections of the poles and quoit. Repeat the procedure with the medium quoit. Use the loppers and pruning shears to trim all the ends of the poles and wands.

DESIGN VARIATIONS

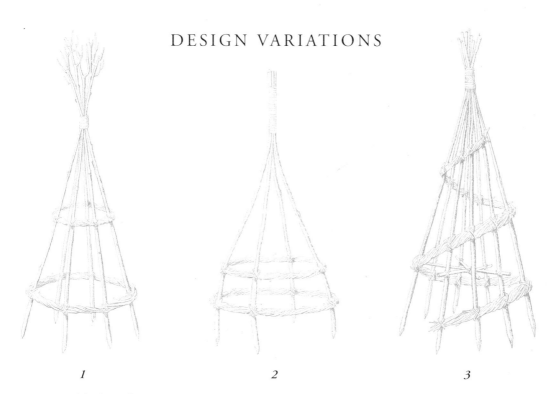

1

2

3

(1) An attractive, natural-looking design incorporating untrimmed twigs at the tops of the poles.

(2) An onion-shaped design with four bent poles. (3) A free-form design braced with a spiral of woven wands.

RUSTIC SLABWOOD GATE

T*his is a copy of a cottage gate that we made when we were doing our best to live self-sufficiently. The original was made from rough-sawed, waney-edged slabwood obtained free from the local sawmill, plus poles donated from a neighbor's copse, all held together with nails. The hinges and the latch were also made from wood.*

YOU WILL NEED

Materials *for a gate approximately 48 in. (1.2 m) high and 27 in. (680 mm) wide.*

☞ Mature beech coppice: 4 posts, $6^1/_2$ ft (2 m) long and 3 in. (80 mm) in diameter (fenceposts)

☞ Beech coppice: 10 poles, 9 ft 9 in. (3 m) long and $1^1/_2$–2 in. (40–50 mm) in diameter (gate hinge rails, fence rails and poles, gate stops)

☞ Rough-sawed hardwood: 3 waney-edged slabs, $6^1/_2$ ft (2 m) long, 8–10 in. (200–250 mm) wide and $^3/_4$–1 in. (20–25 mm) thick (gate uprights and gate ledges)

☞ Beech coppice: 2 forked branches, about 12 in. (300 mm) long and $1^1/_4$–$1^1/_2$ in. (30–40 mm) in diameter (gate latch and catch)

☞ Galvanized nails: 2 lb (1 kg) box of $1^1/_2$ in. (40 mm x 2.65 mm)

☞ Steel nails: 2 lb (1 kg) box of 4 in. (100 mm x 4.5 mm) and 2 lb (1 kg) box of 5 in. (125 mm x 5.6 mm)

☞ Steel washers: 5 washers to fit the 5 in.- (125 mm-) long nails

☞ Two buckets of gravel (or broken brick or rubble)

Tools

☞ Pencil and flexible ruler

☞ Portable workbench

☞ General-purpose, coarse-toothed saw and jigsaw

☞ Small ax

☞ Chopping log

☞ Cordless drill

☞ Wood drill bits to fit the various nail sizes

☞ Claw hammer

☞ Large bevel-edged chisel

☞ Mallet

☞ Spade

☞ Sledgehammer

PERSPECTIVE VIEW OF THE GATE

Gate stop
$1^1/_2$–2 in. (40–50 mm) beech pole, 51 in. (1.3 m) long. Nailed to fencepost so it's flush with the ground

Small gate upright
$^3/_4$–1 in. (20–25 mm) hardwood, 8–10 in. (200–250 mm) wide and 45 in. (1.15 m) long

Gate catch and latch
Forked beech branches

Gate ledge
$^3/_4$–1 in. (20–25 mm) hardwood, 8–10 in. (200–250 mm) wide and 27 in. (680 mm) long

Large gate upright
48 in. (1.2 m) long

Fencepost
3 in. (80 mm) beech post, 51 in. (1.3 m) lon[g]

Gate hinge rail
$1^1/_2$–2 in. (40–50 mm) pole, $29^1/_2$ in. (750 mm) long (extends beyond ga[te] upright by 4 in. [100 [m]

"Clear swing" notch
$2^1/_4$ in. (55 mm) wide, $2^3/_4$ in. (69 mm) deep

Fence pole
$1^1/_2$–2 in. (40–50 mm) pole, 48 in. (1.2 m) lon[g]

Fence rail
$1^1/_2$–2 in. (40–50 mm) pole, $6^1/_2$ ft (2 m) long

HOW TO MAKE THE RUSTIC SLABWOOD GATE

1 Cut the three slabs for the gate uprights. Cut the tops of the slabs to a rough point with the jigsaw. Position the slabs side by side, spacing them to make a total width of 27$\frac{1}{2}$ in. (700 mm).

2 Cut each of the three gate ledges to a length of 27 in. (680 mm). Use the ax to skim the sawed ends to a rough chamfered finish, with the chamfer on the same side as the waney edge.

3 Attach the ledges with 1$\frac{1}{2}$ in. (40 mm) nails (two on one side of the gate to support the hinge rails, and one on the other side). Nail the hinge rails on the other side of the ledges with 1$\frac{1}{2}$ in. (40 mm) nails.

4 Measure and mark two "clear swing" notches on the hinge side of the gate, just below the top hinge rail and just above the bottom hinge rail (as shown on the working drawing). These keep the fence rails from hindering the opening of the gate. Use the saw, chisel, and mallet to remove the waste.

5 Cut the 3 in.- (80 mm-) diameter beech fenceposts to length. Set the gate in position, with temporary poles to hold it upright and to distance it from the ground. Dig holes for the posts, stand them in place, and use the sledgehammer to ram gravel around the posts.

6 Attach the fence rails to the fenceposts, extending them by 4 in. (100 mm) on the hinge side. Attach the poles to the rails, placing them 2 in. (50 mm) above the ground and 2 in. (50 mm) apart. Use 4 in. (100 mm) nails.

7 Rest the top hinge rail on the extended fence rail and drill a $^{7}/_{32}$ in. (5.6 mm) hole through both. Put a washer between them and a nail 5 in. (125 mm) to act as a hinge pin. Repeat for the other hinge.

8 Fashion the catch and latch. Nail the catch to the gatepost, and attach the latch to the gate ledge with a nail and washers. Nail the gate stops to the fenceposts. Use 4 in. (100 mm) nails throughout.

DESIGN VARIATIONS

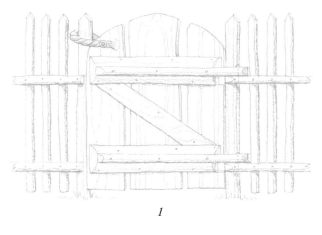

1

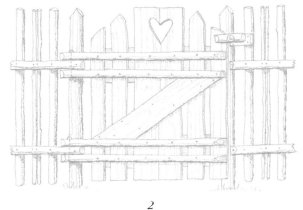

2

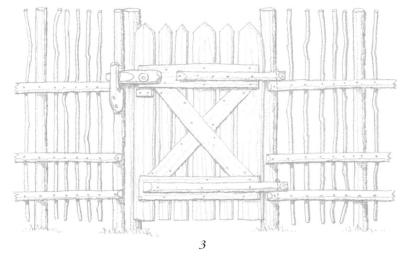

3

(1) A classic design with symmetrical arched top. (2) An American folk art design with heart motif and crossed braces. (3) A traditional English country cottage gate with pointed pickets and crossed braces.

OBELISK

I f you enjoy growing annual climbing plants in the flower or vegetable garden, you will be able to put this project to good use. It will display sweet pea flowers to best advantage, or enable you to grow your runner beans without the need for battalions of sticks. The obelisk is an attractive structure that will enhance your garden, unlike eyesores made from ecologically unfriendly plastic mesh.

YOU WILL NEED

Materials for an obelisk approximately 8 ft (2.5 m) high and 33 in. (830 mm) square.

☞ Hazel coppice: 12 poles, 9 ft 9 in. (3 m) long and 1 in. (25 mm) in diameter (vertical poles)

☞ Beech coppice: 12 rods, 9 ft 9 in. (3 m) long and $^3/_5$ in. (15 mm) in diameter (horizontal ties)

☞ Galvanized wire: small roll of soft $^1/_{16}$ in. (1 mm) wire

Tools

☞ Pencil and flexible ruler

☞ Pruning shears

☞ Pliers

☞ Wire cutters

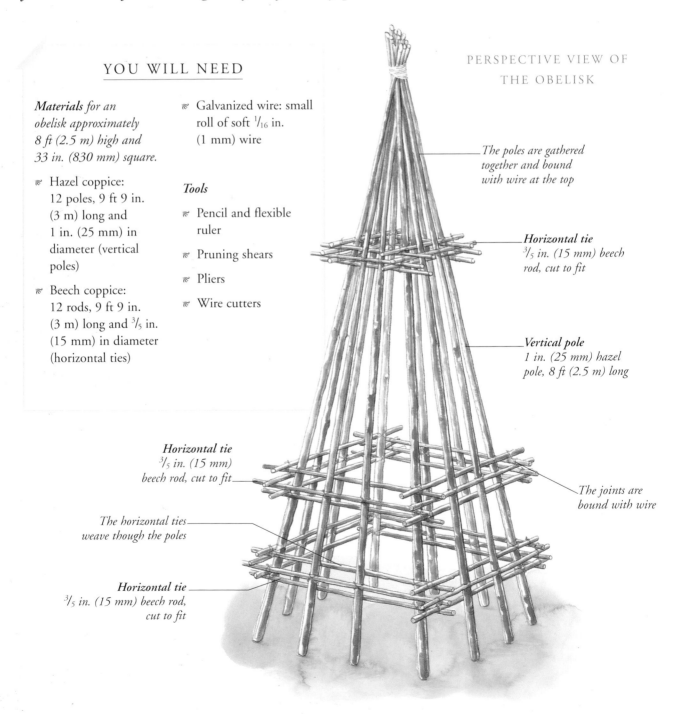

PERSPECTIVE VIEW OF THE OBELISK

The poles are gathered together and bound with wire at the top

Horizontal tie
$^3/_5$ in. (15 mm) beech rod, cut to fit

Vertical pole
1 in. (25 mm) hazel pole, 8 ft (2.5 m) long

The joints are bound with wire

Horizontal tie
$^3/_5$ in. (15 mm) beech rod, cut to fit

The horizontal ties weave though the poles

Horizontal tie
$^3/_5$ in. (15 mm) beech rod, cut to fit

HOW TO MAKE THE OBELISK

1 Cut and trim the twelve hazel vertical poles to a length of 8 ft (2.5 m). Using offcuts to map out the arrangement on the grass, lay two poles on the grass to make an inverted "V" shape, with the heel ends placed about 33 in. (830 mm) apart. To form the horizontal ties, lay beech rods across the "V" at points 12 in., 24 in., and 60 in. (300 mm, 600 mm, and 1.5 m) up from the heel end, and trim them to fit. Bind the intersections with wire.

2 Make another identical frame, then stand them both upright so that the four heels mark out a 33 in. (830 mm) square, and the horizontal tie rods are on the outside of the frame. Cut additional horizontal ties to link the other sides of the two frames, wiring them firmly in place.

3 Stand two more vertical poles against each side of the frame, placing them on the outer side of the horizontal ties. Neighboring poles should be about 11 in. (276 mm) apart at the heels. Wire the vertical poles to the horizontal ties at each intersection, binding them firmly.

4 Weave and wire two more horizontal ties alongside each of those already in place, so that each horizontal bar is made up from three rods. Tighten the wire bindings with pliers until the sticks are pulled close together and the joints are secure.

5 When you are pleased with the obelisk's overall shape, gather the twelve vertical poles at the top and lash them together with wire to hold them tightly. Finally, use the pruning shears to neatly trim the ends of all the poles and rods.

DESIGN VARIATIONS

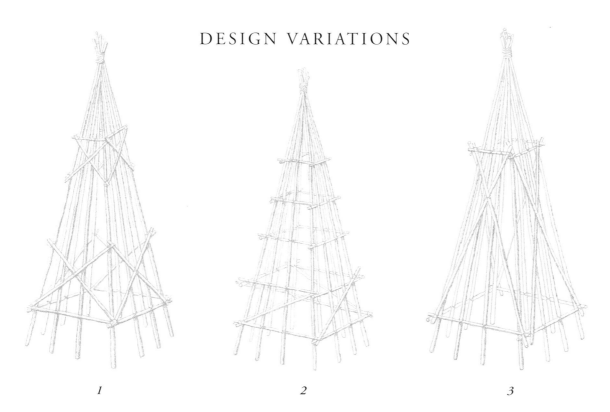

1   *2*   *3*

(1) A traditional design with crossed bracing rods at the sides.
(2) A design with four single diagonal braces at the base, and *horizontal rods. (3) A long-braced design, which creates a strong structure suitable for very windy gardens.*

LOG CABIN PLANTER

With its strong, direct lines, this big, bold planter looks like an American log cabin in miniature. The side panels consist of horizontal cladding poles nailed to corner posts. If you enjoy working with large-section wood, and you would like to build a sturdy container suitable for a large shrub or a small tree, this project is ideal.

YOU WILL NEED

Materials for a planter approximately 31 in. (780 mm) high and 27 in. (700 mm) square.

- ☞ Larch poles with the bark removed: 24 poles, 6$\frac{1}{2}$ ft (2 m) long and 2$\frac{3}{8}$ in. (60 mm) in diameter (for cladding the side panels and floor)

- ☞ Larch poles with the bark removed: 2 poles, 6$\frac{1}{2}$ ft (2 m) long and 3 in. (77 mm) in diameter (corner poles)

- ☞ Beech coppice: 4 rods, 6$\frac{1}{2}$ ft (2 m) long and $\frac{3}{4}$ in. (20 mm) in diameter (decorative motif)

- ☞ Galvanized nails: 1 lb (0.5 kg) box of 1$\frac{1}{2}$ in. (40 mm x 2.65 mm) nails

- ☞ Steel nails: 5 lb (2 kg) box of 5 in. (125 mm x 5.6 mm) nails

Tools

- ☞ Pencil, felt-tip pen, and flexible ruler

- ☞ Crosscut saw

- ☞ Plywood workboard about 60 in. (1.5 m) square

- ☞ Masking tape

- ☞ Electric drill with drill bits to fit your nail sizes

- ☞ Very strong cord or thin rope: about 13 ft (4 m)

- ☞ Claw hammer

- ☞ Long-handled loppers or pruning shears

PERSPECTIVE VIEW OF THE PLANTER

Decorative motif
$\frac{3}{4}$ in. (20 mm) beech rods

Attached with 1$\frac{1}{2}$ in. (40 mm) galvanized nails

First pole is attached 4 in. (100 mm) from the bottom of the corner poles

Corner pole
3 in. (77 mm) larch pole, 31 in. (780 mm) long

Side panel cladding
2$\frac{3}{8}$ in. (60 mm) larch pole, 25 in. (640 mm) long

Attached with 5 in. (125 mm) steel nails

HOW TO MAKE THE LOG CABIN PLANTER

1 Cut 36 identical pieces of cladding, 25 in. (640 mm) long, from the $2^3/_8$ in.- (60 mm-) diameter larch poles. On the plywood workboard, make a simple jig to fit one of the pieces. Place a masking tape marker $1^1/_2$ in. (38 mm) from one end of the jig, and another $3^3/_4$ in. (98 mm) from the other end of the jig. Fit the drill with a bit to match the 5 in. (125 mm) nails, and bore two holes in each cladding pole.

2 Cut the four corner poles. Measure 4 in. (100 mm) up from the foot end of each pole and mark (position of the base). Cut a piece of offcut wood to a length of $16^3/_4$ in. (427 mm), to make a spacer, and use cord to lash it from the top of one corner pole to another. Nail the pre-drilled cladding poles between the two corner poles with 5 in. (125 mm) nails. This forms one side panel.

3 Make another side panel, as described in Step 2. Lash both panels together with the cord and offcut as a spacer, as already described, and nail all the other cladding poles in place with 5 in. (125 mm) nails, completing the other two side panels and forming an open-ended box. Be careful that the spacer doesn't fly free while you are nailing.

4 Cut the remaining $2^3/_8$ in.- (60 mm-) diameter larch poles into lengths of 23 in. (581 mm) for the eleven poles that make the planter's base. Turn the box on its side, so that you are looking into the bottom end. Nail two of the poles to bridge the corner poles, making bearers to support the base. Angle the nails in order to give the base maximum strength.

5 Stand the box on its feet and then drill and nail the other nine poles across the bearers with 5 in. (125 mm) nails. (Two of the poles must be cut to 16³/₄ in. (427 mm) to fit between the corner poles.)

6 Stand the box on its feet and saw the tops of the four corner poles across at an angle to make a decorative face that slopes outward. Trim all pole ends neatly with the loppers.

7 Tip the planter on its side, with the best side up. Using the loppers, cut the beech rods to length for your chosen decorative motif, then attach them with 1¹/₂ in. (40 mm) nails.

DESIGN VARIATIONS

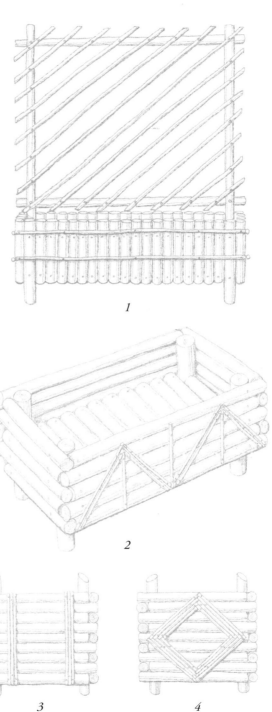

1

2

3

4

(1) A planter with a trellis for climbing plants (the back posts extend upward to form a frame for the trellis). (2) A low planter for holding small plants. (3) A planter with a straightforward vertical stripe motif. (4) A classic planter with a traditional diamond motif.

AMERICAN RUSTIC BENCH

T*here is nothing quite so pleasant as relaxing on a bench that you have made yourself. Drawing inspiration from early American rustic furniture, this bench is easy to make, comfortable to sit on, and good to look at.*

YOU WILL NEED

Materials for a three-seater bench, about 6 1/2 ft (2 m) long.

- Beech mature coppice: 10 poles, 6 1/2 ft (2 m) long and 1 1/2–2 in. (40–50 mm) in diameter (legs, long rails, and diagonal rail to link the ends of the bench, short stretchers to link the legs, diagonal end braces, armrest supports)

- Beech mature coppice: 1 bow-shaped pole, 6 1/2 ft (2 m) long and 2–2 3/8 in. (50–60 mm) in diameter (top rail that forms the curved backrest)

- Beech mature coppice: 2 well-matched poles, 39 in. (1 m) long, which curve and taper from 2 3/8 in. (60 mm) in diameter down to 2 in. (50 mm) (components for the two armrests)

- Hazel or beech bends and forked branches: a selection (decorative apron)

- Hazel coppice: 30 straight rods, 6 1/2 ft (2 m) long and 1–1 1/4 in. (25–30 mm) in diameter (seat, back, and trim rail)

- Steel nails: 2 lb (1 kg) box of 6 in. (150 mm x 6 mm)

- Galvanized cap-end roofing nails: 2 lb (1 kg) box of 3 in. (75 mm)

- Galvanized nails: 2 lb (1 kg) box of 5 in. (125 mm x 5.6 mm), 2 lb (1 kg) box of 4 in. (100 mm x 4 mm)

Tools

- Pencil and flexible ruler

- Portable workbench

- General-purpose, coarse-toothed saw

- Small ax

- Chopping log

- Cordless drill

- Wood bits to fit the various nail sizes

- Claw hammer

- Engineer's hammer

- Long-handled loppers or pruning shears

PERSPECTIVE VIEW OF THE BENCH

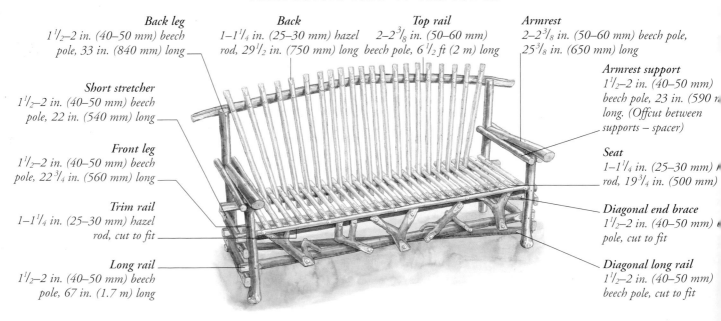

Back leg
1 1/2–2 in. (40–50 mm) beech pole, 33 in. (840 mm) long

Short stretcher
1 1/2–2 in. (40–50 mm) beech pole, 22 in. (540 mm) long

Front leg
1 1/2–2 in. (40–50 mm) beech pole, 22 3/4 in. (560 mm) long

Trim rail
1–1 1/4 in. (25–30 mm) hazel rod, cut to fit

Long rail
1 1/2–2 in. (40–50 mm) beech pole, 67 in. (1.7 m) long

Back
1–1 1/4 in. (25–30 mm) hazel rod, 29 1/2 in. (750 mm) long

Top rail
2–2 3/8 in. (50–60 mm) beech pole, 6 1/2 ft (2 m) long

Armrest
2–2 3/8 in. (50–60 mm) beech pole, 25 3/8 in. (650 mm) long

Armrest support
1 1/2–2 in. (40–50 mm) beech pole, 23 in. (590 m long. (Offcut between supports – spacer)

Seat
1–1 1/4 in. (25–30 mm) rod, 19 3/4 in. (500 mm)

Diagonal end brace
1 1/2–2 in. (40–50 mm) pole, cut to fit

Diagonal long rail
1 1/2–2 in. (40–50 mm) beech pole, cut to fit

HOW TO MAKE THE AMERICAN RUSTIC BENCH

1 Saw the beech poles for the front and back legs to size. Cut the four short stretchers to length, and use the ax to skim the ends to a flat-faced finish. Set the components together, with the stretchers roughly 8 in. (200 mm) apart. Drill pilot holes, and attach the joints with clenched 6 in. (150 mm) nails.

2 Set the two bench ends back to back, square them up by eye, and cut, drill, and nail two diagonal end braces with 4 in. (100 mm) nails, in order to brace and hold the bench ends square. The nails are clenched over tightly on what will be the inside face of the legs.

3 Bridge the bench ends with the four long rails (note flat faces). Drill holes through the rails and legs; attach the joints with clenched nails. Attach the top rail. Use 6 in. (150 mm) nails throughout.

4 Fit the armrest support, using 6 in. (150 mm) nails. Skim a flush top face on the spacer. Drive 6 in. (150 mm) nails through the supports, capturing the spacer. Nail the armrests with 4 in. (100 mm) nails.

5 With the loppers, cut 26 rods, 19$^3/_4$ in. (500 mm) long, for the seat. The back requires 21 rods, 29$^1/_2$ in. (750 mm) long. Use the ax and the chopping log to skim the ends to a flat-faced finish, as shown.

6 Make the seat. Drill and nail the two end rods to the frame with 4 in. (100 mm) nails. Drill and fix the trim rail to the ends of the two rods using cap-end roofing nails. Using one of the seat rods as a spacer, nail the other seat rods to the frame with cap-end roofing nails – so that they are square and the front ends butt on to the trim rail. Place the seat rods so that the best face is up. Trim off any sharp knots.

7 Make the back. Set two back rods in place on either side of the central rod and attach them with roofing nails. Position the other back rods, fanning them out, and attach with roofing nails.

8 Make the decorative apron. Skim the ends of the components to a flat-faced finish; nail to the rails with roofing nails. Attach the diagonal long rail to the legs with clenched 5–6 in. (125–150 mm) nails.

DESIGN VARIATIONS

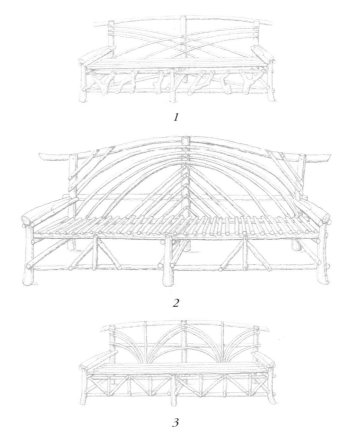

1

2

3

(1) Classic Victorian three-seater design with additional legs at the center.
(2) A design inspired by Chinese motifs, perfect for an oriental-style garden. (3) English Gothic design with pointed arch imagery.

LIVING WILLOW ARCH

B*uilding the living willow arch is a really magical procedure. It starts with a rather flimsy structure made from posts and rods, which is soon transformed into a beautiful, living hedge. It is a wonderfully easy project. We built the framework in late winter, pushed the willow hedgerow cuttings into the ground in early spring, and then we simply watched and waited. The photograph shows the arch after one year's growth.*

YOU WILL NEED

***Materials** for an arch approximately 7 ft (2.15 m) high and 35$\frac{1}{2}$ in. (900 mm) wide, with 6$\frac{1}{2}$ ft (2 m) of fence on either side.*

☞ Larch poles with the bark removed and one end cut to a point: 8 poles, 6$\frac{1}{2}$ ft (2 m) long and 2$\frac{3}{8}$–2$\frac{3}{4}$ in. (60–70 mm) in diameter (uprights)

☞ Beech coppice: 4 rods, 13 ft (4 m) long and $\frac{3}{5}$–$\frac{3}{4}$ in. (15–20 mm) in diameter (arch)

☞ Beech coppice: 8 rods, 9 ft 9 in. (3 m) long and $\frac{3}{5}$–$\frac{3}{4}$ in. (15–20 mm) in diameter (woven horizontal rails)

☞ Willow: 36 cuttings, about 7 in. (180 mm) long

☞ Galvanized nails: 2 lb (1 kg) box of 3 in. (75 mm x 3.75 mm)

☞ Galvanized wire: small roll of soft $\frac{1}{16}$ in. (1 mm) wire

Tools

☞ Pencil and flexible ruler

☞ Sledgehammer

☞ Long-nosed pliers

☞ Stepladder

☞ Claw hammer

☞ Long-handled loppers or pruning shears

PERSPECTIVE VIEW OF THE ARCH

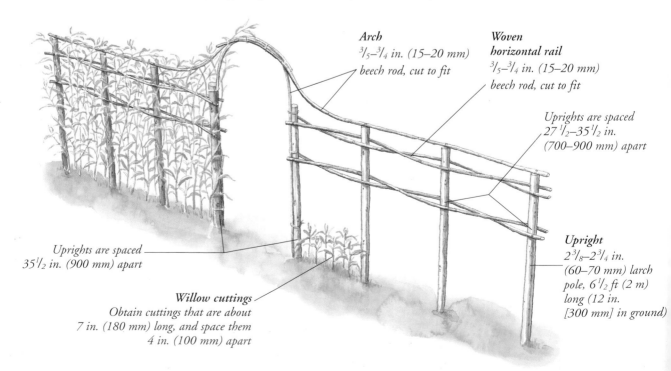

Arch
$\frac{3}{5}$–$\frac{3}{4}$ in. (15–20 mm) beech rod, cut to fit

Woven horizontal rail
$\frac{3}{5}$–$\frac{3}{4}$ in. (15–20 mm) beech rod, cut to fit

Uprights are spaced 27$\frac{1}{2}$–35$\frac{1}{2}$ in. (700–900 mm) apart

Uprights are spaced 35$\frac{1}{2}$ in. (900 mm) apart

Willow cuttings
Obtain cuttings that are about 7 in. (180 mm) long, and space them 4 in. (100 mm) apart

Upright
2$\frac{3}{8}$–2$\frac{3}{4}$ in. (60–70 mm) larch pole, 6$\frac{1}{2}$ ft (2 m) long (12 in. [300 mm] in ground)

HOW TO MAKE THE LIVING WILLOW ARCH

1 Measure out the position of the eight uprights. The archway is 35$\frac{1}{2}$ in. (900 mm) wide, while the other uprights can be set about 27$\frac{1}{2}$–35$\frac{1}{2}$ in. (700–900 mm) apart. Using the sledgehammer, pound the larch poles into the ground to a depth of 12 in. (300 mm), so that the tops are level (judge this by eye).

2 To make the arch, hold two of the 13 ft 1$\frac{1}{2}$ in. (4 m) rods, thin end up, on the inside face of the two uprights for the arch, and wire them in place. Flex the rods repeatedly until they are supple and flexible, then bring them together at top center, making a rounded arch. Wrap the wire at least three times around the overlap.

3 Nail the thick ends of the other two 13 ft 1$\frac{1}{2}$ in. (4 m) rods to the tops of the three outermost uprights on each side. Run the thin ends of the rods in a smooth curve up and over the arch, flexing them and easing them in place. Bind with wire.

4 Weave the eight 9 ft 9 in. (3 m) beech rods in and out of the uprights to make two horizontal rails at either side of the arch. Nail the rods in place and trim the ends with the loppers, so they are flush with the uprights.

5 Trim off the bottom of each willow cutting, to help it establish, and push them into the ground at 4 in. (100 mm) intervals. As the cuttings grow, weave the new growth in and out of the other cuttings and the framework of the arch.

DESIGN VARIATIONS

1

2

3

(1) Linked arches of living willow form an impressive tunnel or curving pergola. (2) An arched framework makes a cozy   *bower or arbor (combined with a green wood bench).*
(3) A living willow wigwam shelter for children to play in.

HEARTS AND DIAMONDS SCREEN

This screen is both functional and decorative. The bottom section is strong enough to hold back pets and children, and the top is high enough to provide shade, give an element of privacy, and support climbing plants. The primary design detail – the heart set within the frame – is very attractive. Another way of using the design is to build several screens and set them side by side to make a fence.

YOU WILL NEED

Materials for a screen approximately 74 in. (1.88 m) high and 53¹/₂ in. (1.36 m) wide.

- Larch poles: 6 de-barked poles, 6½ ft (2 m) long and 2³/₈ in. (60 mm) in diameter (main frame)

- Beech coppice: 80 rods, 6½ ft (2 m) long and ²/₅–³/₄ in. (10–20 mm) in diameter (woven lower section, heart shape, and diamond lattice)

- Galvanized nails: 2 lb (1 kg) box of 3 in. (75 mm x 3.75 mm)

- Steel nails: 2 lb (1 kg) box of 5 in. (125 mm x 5.6 mm)

- Galvanized wire: small roll of soft ¹/₁₆ in. (1 mm) wire

Tools

- Pencil and flexible ruler

- Two portable workbenches

- General-purpose, coarse-toothed saw

- Mallet

- Bevel-edged chisel, 1½–2 in. (40–50 mm) wide

- Claw hammer

- Long-nosed pliers

- Long handled loppers or pruning shears

PERSPECTIVE VIEW
OF THE SCREEN

Heart
²/₅–³/₄ in. (10–20 mm) beech rods, cut to fit

Main frame vertical
2³/₈ in. (60 mm) larch pole, 74 in. (1.88 m) long

Diamond lattice
²/₅–³/₄ in. (10–20 mm) beech rods, cut to fit

Woven lower section
²/₅–³/₄ in. (10–20 mm) beech rods, cut to fit

Main frame horizontal
2³/₈ in. (60 mm) larch pole, 53¹/₂ in. (1.36 m) long

HOW TO MAKE THE HEARTS AND DIAMONDS SCREEN

1 Cut the six larch poles for the main frame to length: three verticals at 74 in. (1.88 m) long and three horizontals at 53½ in. (1.36 m). To make the lap joints, measure 6¼ in. (160 mm) along from the ends of all the poles and saw halfway through the 2⅜ in. (60 mm) diameter. Run the saw cut so that it angles toward the end of the pole.

2 Once you have sawed halfway through the diameter, take the mallet and chisel and chop directly into the end of the pole, so that the split travels into the saw cut and the waste falls away. For the central laps, make two angled saw cuts and clear the waste wood by slicing, at a low angle, into the cuts.

3 Lay the three vertical poles parallel on the grass, with the cut-away sections up. Place the horizontal poles in position so that all the joints are aligned, and then hammer one 5 in. (125 mm) nail through each intersection. Turn the frame over and pound the points of the nails over and back down into the wood to clench the joints tight.

4 Take about 50 of the thickest beech rods and weave them alternately in and out of the three vertical poles, to make up the panel at the bottom of the frame. Select the wood carefully so that neighboring rods fit together snugly. Use the mallet to pack the rods tight and to pound the ends level. Nail the ends with 3 in. (75 mm) nails.

5 Nail beech rods diagonally across the top of the frame with 3 in. (75 mm) nails, to form one side of the lattice. Turn it over so that the lattice is on the underside. Bind three of the thinner beech rods together with wire, then ease them into the top of the frame to form a portion of the heart shape. Wire it to the main frame. Repeat this procedure to finish the heart motif.

6 Nail another set of rods in place with 3 in. (75 mm) nails, so that they cross the first set, and so that the bundles of rods making up the heart are contained. If necessary, use additional wire binding to hold the bundles in place. Trim the ends of all the rods to a neat finish with the loppers or pruning shears. Stand the screen in position and push the verticals into the ground.

DESIGN VARIATIONS

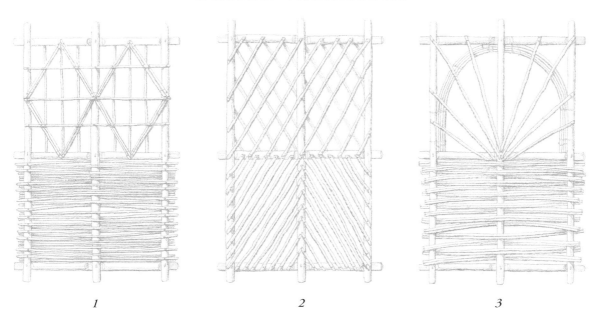

1

2

3

(1) A traditional design incorporating diamond motifs at the top. (2) A design that negates the need to weave the rods – the pattern is formed by nailed rods. (3) A classic design that uses a Roman arch motif at the top of the screen.

RUSTIC PAVILION PERGOLA

O*ne of the quickest ways of creating a large design statement in a garden is to build a pergola. Pergolas are versatile – depending on its size and strength, a pergola can be a frame for your grapevines, the central feature of your rose garden, a place for a swing, a pavilion over your barbecue area, or whatever else inspires you.*

YOU WILL NEED

Materials *for a pergola approximately 6 ft 10 in. (2.1 m) high, 6¹/₂ ft (2 m) wide, and 12 ft 1¹/₂ in. (3.7 m) long.*

- Marking sticks: 6 short sticks

- Larch posts: 6 posts, 9 ft 9 in. (3 m) long and 4 in. (100 mm) in diameter (vertical posts)

- Larch posts: 8 posts, 6¹/₂ ft (2 m) long and 4 in. (100 mm) in diameter (main beams, banister rails, footrails)

- Larch posts: 7 posts, 6¹/₂ ft (2 m) long and 3 in. (80 mm) in diameter (rafters)

- Beech mature coppice: 3 poles, 9 ft 9 in. (3 m) long and 2 in. (50 mm) in diameter (diagonal braces)

- Hazel coppice: 11 rods, 9 ft 9 in. (3 m) long and ³/₄–1 in. (20–25 mm) in diameter (decorative balustrade)

- Steel nails: 2 lb (1 kg) box of 6 in. (150 mm x 6 mm), 2 lb (1 kg) box of 4 in. (100 mm x 4.5 mm)

- Gravel: 6 buckets

- Temporary braces: 2 poles, about 6¹/₂ ft (2 m) long (for setting up the pergola)

Tools

- Pencil and flexible ruler

- Ball of twine

- Engineer's hammer

- Spade

- Sledgehammer

- Stepladder

- Measuring board, 6¹/₂ ft (2 m) long

- General-purpose, coarse-toothed saw

- Spirit level

- Two portable workbenches

- Small ax

- Cordless drill

- Drill bits to fit the size of your nails

- Claw hammer

- Long-handled loppers or pruning shears

PERSPECTIVE VIEW OF THE PERGOLA

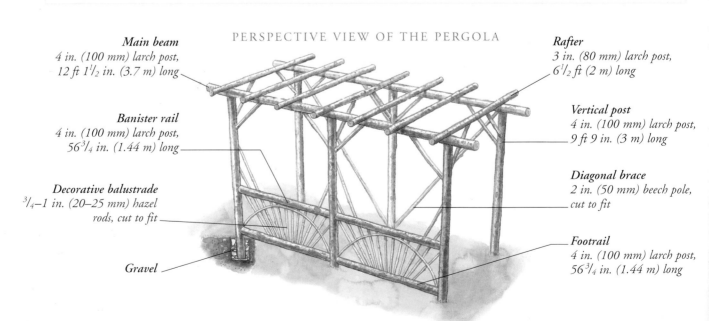

Main beam
4 in. (100 mm) larch post, 12 ft 1¹/₂ in. (3.7 m) long

Banister rail
4 in. (100 mm) larch post, 56³/₄ in. (1.44 m) long

Decorative balustrade
³/₄–1 in. (20–25 mm) hazel rods, cut to fit

Gravel

Rafter
3 in. (80 mm) larch post, 6¹/₂ ft (2 m) long

Vertical post
4 in. (100 mm) larch post, 9 ft 9 in. (3 m) long

Diagonal brace
2 in. (50 mm) beech pole, cut to fit

Footrail
4 in. (100 mm) larch post, 56³/₄ in. (1.44 m) long

HOW TO MAKE THE RUSTIC PAVILION PERGOLA

1 Use the ruler, twine, engineer's hammer, and marking sticks to establish the position of the six vertical posts. Set the three front posts 59 in. (1.5 m) apart, the three back posts likewise, with the aisle between them measuring 51 in. (1.3 m). Check that the diagonal measurements are identical.

2 Dig a hole, 12 in. (300 mm) deep, for each vertical post. Fill the hole with 4 in. (100 mm) of gravel, stand the post on it and prop it up with the temporary braces. Pack more gravel into the hole, compacting it with the sledgehammer and engineer's hammer. Set all six vertical posts in place.

3 Use the measuring board to establish a point 6½ ft (2 m) above ground level on one vertical post. Saw through the post at this point. Cut the tops of the other five posts level with this.

4 Cut a 4 in.- (100 mm-) long half-lap on one end of each main beam. Mark 4 in. (100 mm) from the end, saw halfway through the post's diameter, and remove the waste with the ax.

5 Position the main beams on top of the vertical posts, centering the lap joints on the middle posts. Attach in place with 6 in. (150 mm) nails (drill pilot holes to avoid splitting the wood).

6 Position the rafters on top of the beams, directly above the central vertical posts, and attach with 6 in. (150 mm) nails. Make sure that all the rafters are square to the main beams and parallel.

7 Using a saw, hammer, and 6 in. (150 mm) nails, attach the banister and footrails to the three front vertical posts: footrails 4 in. (100 mm) above ground level; banisters 31½ in. (800 mm) above ground level.

8 Make the diagonal braces: the 24 in.-(600 mm-) long braces between the vertical posts, main beams, and rafters, and the two that link the three back vertical posts. Attach with 4 in. (100 mm) nails.

9 Use the eleven hazel coppice rods to make the decorative balustrading – the two curved bows, and the rods that fan out from the center of the two footrails. Use 4 in. (100 mm) nails to fix the rods in place. Finally, use the loppers and saw to trim all the wood to a neat finish.

DESIGN VARIATIONS

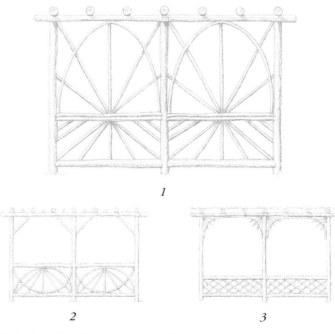

1

2   *3*

(1) A classic arched design with a sunburst pattern. (2) A design featuring double curves under the banister. (3) An American folk art design with "gingerbread" brackets and a diamond pattern border.

COUNTRY CLUB CHAIR

T*his beautifully curvaceous chair draws its inspiration from the generously large porch and loggia armchairs our family used to have back in the late 1950s. This chair is surprisingly easy to build. All you do is set up the four-square frame, and then bend the wands around and down to make the arms and back.*

YOU WILL NEED

Materials for a chair approximately 33¼ in. (845 mm) high, 27½ in. (700 mm) wide, and 34 in. (865 mm) deep.

☞ Beech mature coppice: 6 poles, 9 ft 9 in. (3 m) long and 1½–2 in. (40–50 mm) in diameter (legs, rails, and diagonal stretchers)

☞ Beech coppice: 1 rod, 9 ft 9 in. (3 m) long and ⅗–¾ in. (15–20 mm) in diameter (rail bracers)

☞ Beech coppice: 10 rods, 6½ ft (2 m) long and 1–1¼ in. (25–30 mm) in diameter (seat, back, and seat trim pieces)

☞ Beech coppice: 20 wands, 9 ft 9 in. (3 m) long and ⅖–⅗ in. (10–15 mm) in diameter (arms, backrest, and decorative underarm detail)

☞ Galvanized cap-end roofing nails: 2 lb (1 kg) box of 3 in. (75 mm)

☞ Galvanized nails: 2 lb (1 kg) box of 4 in. (100 mm x 4.5 mm), 2 lb (1 kg) box of 3 in. (75 mm x 3.75 mm), 2 lb (1 kg) box of 1½ in. (40 mm x 2.65 mm)

Tools

☞ Pencil, flexible ruler, and square

☞ Portable workbench

☞ General-purpose, coarse-toothed saw

☞ Small ax

☞ Chopping log

☞ Plywood workboard about 60 in. (1.5 m) square

☞ Cordless drill

☞ Wood bits to fit the various nail sizes

☞ Claw hammer

☞ Long-handled loppers

☞ Pruning shears

PERSPECTIVE VIEW OF THE CHAIR

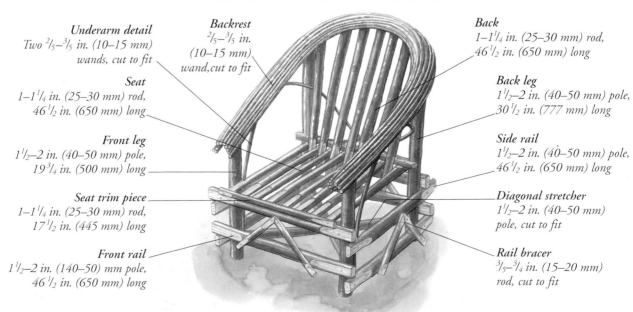

Underarm detail
Two ⅖–⅗ in. (10–15 mm) wands, cut to fit

Seat
1–1¼ in. (25–30 mm) rod, 46½ in. (650 mm) long

Front leg
1½–2 in. (40–50 mm) pole, 19¾ in. (500 mm) long

Seat trim piece
1–1¼ in. (25–30 mm) rod, 17½ in. (445 mm) long

Front rail
1½–2 in. (140–50) mm pole, 46½ in. (650 mm) long

Backrest
⅖–⅗ in. (10–15 mm) wand, cut to fit

Back
1–1¼ in. (25–30 mm) rod, 46½ in. (650 mm) long

Back leg
1½–2 in. (40–50 mm) pole, 30½ in. (777 mm) long

Side rail
1½–2 in. (40–50 mm) pole, 46½ in. (650 mm) long

Diagonal stretcher
1½–2 in. (40–50 mm) pole, cut to fit

Rail bracer
⅗–¾ in. (15–20 mm) rod, cut to fit

HOW TO MAKE THE COUNTRY CLUB CHAIR

1 Saw all the straight members for the chair to length – everything except the wood that is to be bent (the beech coppice wands that make the backrest). Use the ax to skim flat faces on the ends of the rails and rail bracers, and the rods that make the seat.

2 Set two legs, two rails, and two rail bracers flat on the workboard, so that they make one side of the chair. The legs should be 18 in. (460 mm) apart on the inside edges. Make checks with the square, drill pilot holes through the topmost rods, and attach with 4 in. (100 mm) nails.

3 Make the other side. Each side of the chair is a mirror image copy of the other. Connect them with the rails and rail bracers. The chair sides should be 17½ in. (445 mm) apart on the inside edges.

4 Cut the diagonal stretchers to a very tight push-fit and nail them in place with 3 in. (75 mm) nails, with the nails running from the ends of the stretchers and into the legs.

5 Make the seat. Arrange the seat rods from front to back of the chair. Attach to the top of the rails. Nail a trim piece to cover the front ends of the rods. Use roofing nails throughout.

6 Nail a second trim piece across the seat rods, so that it butts hard up against the two back legs. One at a time, bend and nail the backrest wands to the top of the legs with 1½ in. (40 mm) nails.

7 Position the seat back rods, nailing the bottom ends to the trim piece. Fan out the rods and nail the top ends through the curved wands. Use 3 in. (75 mm) nails throughout.

8 Attach the underarm detail wands (inside the front legs, under the arms, around the back to the back rails). Attach eight wands to make the back and arm shape. Use 1½ in. (40 mm) nails throughout.

DESIGN VARIATIONS

1

2

3

(1) Traditional American folk art design with "twisted ribbon" arms.
(2) Bow-backed design with naturally bent rustic legs and an extra-wide seat. (3) High-backed design complemented by "ribbon" arms.

CANTILEVER BRIDGE

I*f you want to create a really big, impressive project, you can't do much better than this bridge, which is a lot of fun to build. If the idea of living the life of a pioneer, building log cabins and suspension bridges over river canyons, appeals to you, this project will give you a taste of what it was like to be an early American settler.*

YOU WILL NEED

Materials for a bridge approximately 71 in. (1.8 m) high, 51 in. (1.3 m) wide, and 12 ft (3.7 m) long.

☞ Larch: 2 straight young trees, 14 ft (4 m) long and 5 in. (130 mm) in diameter (two main beams)

☞ Larch: 2 posts, 6½ ft (2 m) long and 5 in. (130 mm) in diameter (four piles)

☞ Larch: 5 posts, 9 ft 9 in. (3 m) long and 4 in. (100 mm) in diameter (walkway surface)

☞ Larch: 3 posts, 6½ ft (2 m) long and 4 in. (100 mm) in diameter (walkway cantilevers)

☞ Beech mature coppice: 4 bow-shaped poles, 14 ft (4 m) long and 1½–2 in. (40–50 mm) in diameter (banister rails)

☞ Beech mature coppice: 6 poles, 9 ft 9 in. (3 m) long and 1½–2 in. (40–50 mm) in diameter (rail supports)

☞ Beech mature coppice: 4 poles, 6½ ft (2 m) long and 1½–2 in. (40–50 mm) in diameter (rail support braces)

☞ Steel nails: 5 lb (2 kg) box of 5 in. (125 mm x 5.6 mm), 5 lb (2 kg) box of 6 in. (150 mm x 6 mm)

Tools

☞ Pencil and flexible ruler

☞ Portable workbench

☞ General-purpose, coarse-toothed saw

☞ Small ax

☞ Chopping log

☞ Sledgehammer

☞ Cordless drill

☞ Wood bits to fit the various nail sizes

☞ Mallet

☞ Claw hammer

PERSPECTIVE VIEW
OF THE BRIDGE

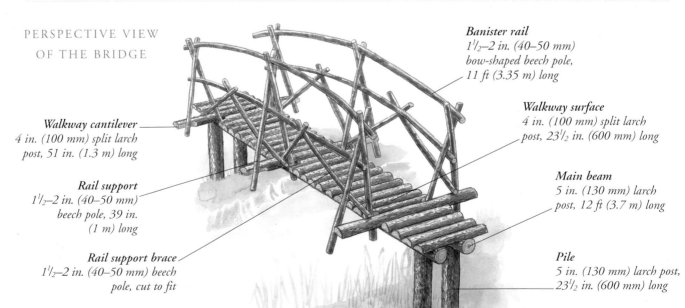

Banister rail
1½–2 in. (40–50 mm)
bow-shaped beech pole,
11 ft (3.35 m) long

Walkway cantilever
4 in. (100 mm) split larch
post, 51 in. (1.3 m) long

Rail support
1½–2 in. (40–50 mm)
beech pole, 39 in.
(1 m) long

Rail support brace
1½–2 in. (40–50 mm) beech
pole, cut to fit

Walkway surface
4 in. (100 mm) split larch
post, 23½ in. (600 mm) long

Main beam
5 in. (130 mm) larch
post, 12 ft (3.7 m) long

Pile
5 in. (130 mm) larch post,
23½ in. (600 mm) long

HOW TO MAKE THE CANTILEVER BRIDGE

1 Saw the four piles to length at 23½ in. (600 mm) long, and use the ax to shape the ends into a point. Pair the piles 5½ in. (140 mm) apart – positioning them at either side of the pond – and pound them into the ground with the sledge-hammer, so that the top ends are level with each other. Drill and nail the two main beams in place with 6 in. (150 mm) nails.

2 Cut the walkway surface posts and cantilevers to length; use the ax and mallet to split them in half. Position the cantilevers four logs in at each end, and one in the center. Ax away part of the ends of three walkway pieces to accommodate the rail supports. Nail the walkway surface posts and cantilevers across the two main beams using 5 in. (125 mm) nails.

3 Cut the twelve rail supports to length at 39 in. (1 m) long, and arrange them in well-matched pairs. Take one pair of supports at a time and drill, nail, and clench them at a point about 8 in. (200 mm) along from the end, so as to make an "X" shape. Use 6 in. (150 mm) nails.

4 Set the crossed rail supports in position, so that they are at the correct height (top end about 25¾ in. [655 mm] above the walkway surface), balanced, and with the intersection at the top. Drill and nail them to the extended ends of the walkway cantilevers, using 6 in. (150 mm) nails.

5 Set the top banister rails in place so that they are cupped by the top of the crossed rail supports, and attach them with clenched 6 in. (150 mm) nails. You will need help to bend and ease the rails into place. Attach the lower banister rails on the underside of the crossed rail supports with 5 in. (125 mm) nails.

6 Cut the eight rail support braces to length and nail the bottom ends to the bottom of the crossed rail supports, and the top ends to the middle of the lower banister rails. Use 5 in. (125 mm) nails. To give the structure extra strength, clench over the nails on the outside of the rails.

DESIGN VARIATIONS

1

2

3

(1) *A design including steps leading down a sloping bank to a bridge.* *(2)* *Traditional design with curved handrail and twisted rail details.* *(3)* *This design draws its inspiration from the images on Chinese willow pattern china.*

"TEA FOR TWO" SHELTER

P*icture yourself and a companion whiling away a warm summer's afternoon in this shaded shelter, with a pitcher of iced tea for two. What could be more delightful? The shelter also provides a place to enjoy the garden throughout the seasons.*

YOU WILL NEED

Materials for a shelter approximately 11 ft 6 in. (3.5 m) high and 67 in. (1.7 m) in diameter.

☞ Larch : 16 posts, 9 ft 9 in. (3 m) long and 5$\frac{1}{2}$ in. (140 mm) in diameter (six vertical posts, horizontal rails, and roof finial)

☞ Larch: 3 posts, 6$\frac{1}{2}$ ft (2 m) long and 4 in. (100 mm) in diameter (floor joists)

☞ Larch: 6 twisted decorative poles, 6$\frac{1}{2}$ ft (2 m) long and 1$\frac{1}{2}$–2$\frac{3}{8}$ in. (40–60 mm) in diameter (decorative banister rails)

☞ Beech mature coppice: 3 poles, 6$\frac{1}{2}$ ft (2 m) long and 2$\frac{3}{8}$ in. (60 mm) in diameter (roof rafters)

☞ Beech mature coppice: 8 poles, 6$\frac{1}{2}$ ft (2 m) long and 1$\frac{1}{2}$ in. (40 mm) in diameter (roof ties, diagonal wall braces, and wall brackets)

☞ Hazel coppice: 9 rods, 6$\frac{1}{2}$ ft (2 m) long and $\frac{3}{4}$–1 in. (20–25 mm) in diameter (roof and wall trim, straight banister rails)

☞ Sawed boards: 10 treated boards, 6$\frac{1}{2}$ ft (2 m) long, 6 in. (150 mm) wide and $\frac{3}{4}$ in. (20 mm) thick (floorboards and sills)

☞ Feather-edge cladding (rough-sawed): 7 in. x 6$\frac{1}{2}$ ft (180 mm x 2 m) long, 4 in. (100 mm) wide, and $\frac{2}{5}$ in. (10 mm) thick (three back walls and roof, felt supports)

☞ Steel nails: 6$\frac{1}{2}$ lb (3 kg) box of 6 in. (150 mm x 6 mm), 5 lb (2 kg) box of 5 in. (125 mm x 5.6 mm), 5 lb (2 kg) box of 4 in. (100 mm x 4.5 mm)

☞ Galvanized nails: 5 lb (2 kg) box of 1$\frac{1}{2}$ in. (40 mm x 2.65 mm)

☞ Concrete blocks/slabs: 6 or more (post pads)

☞ Plastic sheeting: a piece of medium-grade plastic sheeting, about 10 ft (3 m) square

☞ Roofing felt: 1 roll of medium-grade roofing felt, 39 in. (1 m) wide and 30 ft (10 m) long

☞ Flashing: 6$\frac{1}{2}$ ft (2 m) self-adhesive flashing, 12 in. (300 mm) wide

Tools

☞ Pencil, felt-tip pen, and flexible ruler

☞ Two portable workbenches

☞ General-purpose, coarse-toothed saw

☞ Mallet

☞ Large chisel

☞ Cordless drill

☞ Drill bits to fit the size of your nails

☞ Claw hammer

☞ Ball of twine

☞ Spirit level and 6$\frac{1}{2}$ ft (2 m) length of board

☞ Stepladder

☞ Small ax

☞ Craft knife and a pair of old scissors

☞ Long-handled loppers

☞ Pruning shears

PERSPECTIVE VIEW
OF THE SHELTER

EXPLODED VIEW OF THE SHELTER

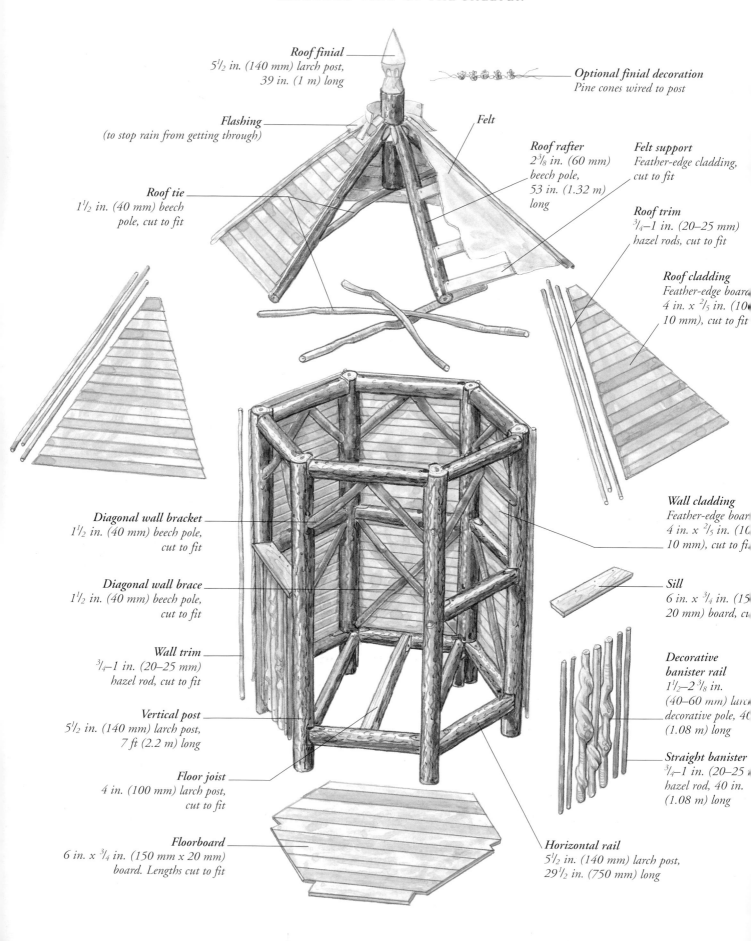

Roof finial
*5¹⁄₂ in. (140 mm) larch post,
39 in. (1 m) long*

Optional finial decoration
Pine cones wired to post

Flashing
(to stop rain from getting through)

Felt

Roof rafter
*2³⁄₈ in. (60 mm)
beech pole,
53 in. (1.32 m)
long*

Felt support
*Feather-edge cladding,
cut to fit*

Roof tie
*1¹⁄₂ in. (40 mm) beech
pole, cut to fit*

Roof trim
*³⁄₄–1 in. (20–25 mm)
hazel rods, cut to fit*

Roof cladding
*Feather-edge board
4 in. x ²⁄₅ in. (10
10 mm), cut to fit*

Wall cladding
*Feather-edge board
4 in. x ²⁄₅ in. (10
10 mm), cut to fi*

Diagonal wall bracket
*1¹⁄₂ in. (40 mm) beech pole,
cut to fit*

Diagonal wall brace
*1¹⁄₂ in. (40 mm) beech pole,
cut to fit*

Sill
*6 in. x ³⁄₄ in. (15
20 mm) board, cu*

Wall trim
*³⁄₄–1 in. (20–25 mm)
hazel rod, cut to fit*

**Decorative
banister rail**
*1¹⁄₂–2³⁄₈ in.
(40–60 mm) larc
decorative pole, 40
(1.08 m) long*

Vertical post
*5¹⁄₂ in. (140 mm) larch post,
7 ft (2.2 m) long*

Straight banister
*³⁄₄–1 in. (20–25
hazel rod, 40 in.
(1.08 m) long*

Floor joist
*4 in. (100 mm) larch post,
cut to fit*

Floorboard
*6 in. x ³⁄₄ in. (150 mm x 20 mm)
board. Lengths cut to fit*

Horizontal rail
*5¹⁄₂ in. (140 mm) larch post,
29¹⁄₂ in. (750 mm) long*

HOW TO MAKE THE "TEA FOR TWO" SHELTER

1 Cut the six vertical posts. Use the diagram to mark the position of the rails at roof, banister, and floor level. Cut out the housings (at an angle of 60°) for the ends of the horizontal rails.

2 Pair the vertical posts on the grass. Nail the nine horizontal rails (ends angled back at 60°) in place. Attach the wall brackets across the top corners. Use 6 in. (150 mm) nails throughout.

3 Level the site and cover with plastic sheet. Draw a circle with a radius of 33½ in. (850 mm). Lay a concrete block for each vertical post (make sure they are at more or less the same level).

4 Set the paired vertical posts on the concrete blocks (make sure the entrance is facing in the correct direction) and use temporary props to hold them in place. Link the posts with the remaining horizontal rails. Use the spirit level to ensure that the posts are upright.

5 Set the the two outer floor joists in place, supported on offcuts and nailed to the posts, also the middle joist (housed at front and back, and nailed to the rails). Use 6 in. (150 mm) nails. Note how the middle housing is lapped to take the downward thrust of the weight of the floor.

6 Nail the floorboards across the joists with 4 in. (100 mm) nails. Work from the front of the shelter to the back, so that the doorstep is made from a single complete board width.

7 Set three of the most bowed roof tie poles across the walls, so that they go over and under each other to link opposite vertical posts. Nail to the top of the posts with 4 in. (100 mm) nails.

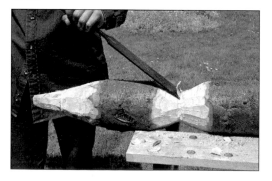

8 Cut the roof finial to length and use the saw, mallet, and chisel to cut a ring housing for the end of the rafters. Sculpt the top of the post to a decorative point with the ax.

9 Build a roof A-frame with the finial post, two of the rafters, and a length of beech offcut. Position the frame to span the walls, propping it upright with a temporary stay. Nail the A-frame to the top of the vertical posts and then attach the other four rafters in place. Use 5 in. (125 mm) nails.

10 Nail lengths of feather-edge cladding across the roof, to support the roofing felt. With craft knife and scissors, cut the roofing felt to size. One triangle at a time, and starting at the bottom, cover the roof with sheets of overlapping felt. Cut and attach the cladding, flashing, and pine cones.

11 Starting just above ground level, cut the cladding to length and drill and nail it in place across the outside of the three back bays, or panels, using 1½ in. (40 mm) nails. Position the cladding so that the waney edge is displayed. Do your best to center the ends of the cladding, or the sides of neighboring panels, so that they meet in a straight line on the posts.

12 Finally, when you have cut and fitted the two sills, the various diagonal wall braces, and the roof trim that covers the ends of the cladded roof and wall panels, use the twisted decorative poles and hazel rods to make the decorative banister rails and straight banister rails. Nail in position with 4 in. (100 mm) nails. Trim the ends with the loppers and pruning shears.

DESIGN VARIATIONS

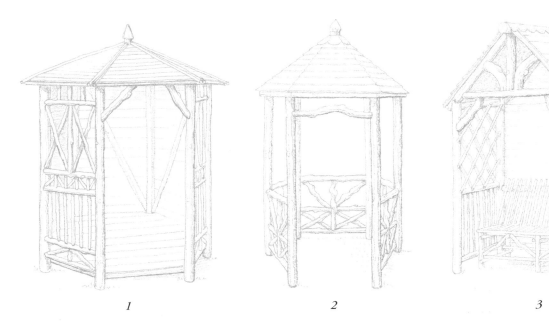

1

2

3

(1) A design featuring a low roof, suitable for exposed windy sites. (2) An open-sided design, intended to encourage climbing plants to cover the sides. (3) A rectangular shelter or arbor with lattice sides and a lovers' seat inside.

SUPPLIERS

Consult the telephone directory for details of local wood suppliers. Other materials such as nails, wire, and twine, and all the tools featured in this book, are available from home improvement stores.

Tool suppliers
Mytoolstore.com
www.mytoolstore.com
Contains hand and power tools, on-line shopping, expert advice.

The Stanley Works
www.stanleyworks.com
Site contains information about tools and where to purchase them.

The Tool Barn
www.thetoolbarn.com
Features hand tools for woodworkers, on-line shopping.

Hardware suppliers
The Hardware and Home Center Industry Resource Center
http://www.nrha.org/LINKS.html
Provides source for consumers to find hardware and related sites.

Restoration Hardware
www.restoration-hardware.com
Contains hardware, customer service, and store locator.

Home improvement centers
Inside Spaces
www.insidespaces.com
Features how-to projects and tool dictionary.

Home & Workshop Online
www.johathanpress.com
Contains advertisers, links, and woodworking plans.

Lowe's Home Improvement Warehouse
www.lowes.com
Contains how-to library, on-line shopping, customer service, and store locator.

Wood suppliers
CyberYard Online Resources
www.cyberyard.com
Features wood library, terms glossary, ask the pros, resources.

Eco Timber
www.ecotimber.com
Distributor of ecological forest products. Site contains products, services, and sources.

EZ Wood
www.ezewood.com
Contains projects, on-line shopping catalogues, and links. Suppliers for hobbyists, carvers, and small woodworking shops.

INDEX